Enhancing Teacher Performance

Enhancing Teacher Performance

A Toolbox of Strategies to Facilitate Moving Behavior from Problematic to Good and from Good to Great

W. George Selig, Linda D. Grooms,
Alan A. Arroyo, Michael D. Kelly,
Glenn L. Koonce and Herman D. Clark Jr.

ROWMAN & LITTLEFIELD
Lanham • Boulder • New York • London

Published by Rowman & Littlefield
A wholly owned subsidiary of The Rowman & Littlefield Publishing Group, Inc.
4501 Forbes Boulevard, Suite 200, Lanham, Maryland 20706
www.rowman.com

Unit A, Whitacre Mews, 26-34 Stannary Street, London SE11 4AB

British Library Cataloguing in Publication Information Available

Library of Congress Cataloging-in-Publication Data
Names: Selig, W. George, author.
Title: Enhancing teacher performance : a toolbox of strategies to facilitate moving behavior
    from problematic to good and from good to great / W. George Selig, Linda D. Grooms,
    Alan A. Arroyo, Michael D. Kelly, Glenn L. Koonce and Herman D. Clark Jr.
Description: Lanham, Maryland : Rowman & Littlefield, 2016. | Includes bibliographical
    references.
Identifiers: LCCN 2015040974 | ISBN 9781475817874 (cloth : alk. paper) | ISBN 9781475817881
    (pbk. : alk. paper) | ISBN 9781475817898 (electronic)
Subjects: LCSH: Educational leadership—United States. | Teacher effectiveness—United States. |
    School personnel management—United States.
Classification: LCC LB2805 .S497 2016 | DDC 371.2/011—dc23
LC record available at http://lccn.loc.gov/2015040974

Contents

Preface

Successful and, more importantly exemplary schools have at their core outstanding principals and teachers. In this book, it is our goal to propose what enables principals to move teacher behavior from *problematic to good*, or better yet what Jim Collins (2001) so eloquently refers to as *good to great*. While we provide insights, suggestions, and very specific strategies that can be used by school leaders to encourage and promote essential teacher qualities, we also provide intervention techniques that will lead to improvement of many of the problematic issues that have for years been the bane of principals.

Serving as a reference tool, this book introduces both general and specific leadership principles to develop a culture of teacher and consequently student success. However, while developing a positive school culture is a necessary step to this success, principals must often work with teachers on an individual basis to facilitate continued growth and increased productivity. There are a plethora of day-to-day teacher-related issues that must be faced ranging from absenteeism to inadequate writing skills and administrators need a set of constructs and an array of tools in order to face those daily challenges.

In developing the Individualized Intervention Strategy System (IISS), we borrowed heavily from our previous works in the areas of classroom management, resilience, character development, parenting, and communication skill building. We then combined our extensive experience as building and school district administrators to design various strategies to meet a myriad of problematic behaviors. We further validated these strategies with additional seasoned school leaders who currently serve in K-12 administrative posts.

We begin this work in chapter 1 by establishing the importance of the principal-teacher relationship. Chapter 2 follows offering some general challenges the principal may face but if handled correctly can be used to facilitate an open, caring, and positive school climate and culture. In chapters 3 and 4, we introduce four stages of motivational development and four behavioral styles, which are at the core of our IISS. Once the core is established, in chapter 5 we highlight four skill clusters of quality teaching and how those relate specifically to motivation stage and behavior style. In chapter 6, we move deeper into the IISS by providing a list of specific problematic issues that often arise. These 38 common challenges serve as a starting point as you begin to use the system. Once an issue is identified, the principal will assess the stage of motivation

viii   *Preface*

and the behavior style of the teacher to best select from one of the 304 strategies most likely to be effective in correcting the attitude or behavior in chapters 7–9. We conclude in chapter 10 by providing two case studies to show the IISS in action. The goal is to raise the capacity of a teacher by identifying the problem behaviors and matching them with intervention strategies ranging from slightly to extremely intrusive. Each of the first seven chapters concludes with reflective questions to ponder.

It is our hope that this material can be used on the run so to speak so that you, the principal, can effectively intervene in any situation with a variety of strategies available to you and have even more in reserve if necessary. Many school leaders have told us that this book is an easy reference that dramatically increases their understanding of teacher behavior and exponentially increases the number of strategies and techniques available to them when dealing with challenging situations.

In summary, this book not only helps principals look at themselves in terms of their leadership abilities, but also helps them look at their strengths and weaknesses in working with teachers. It provides a way forward for those principals who desire to create an encouraging and redemptive milieu in their schools, working alongside the teachers in a true partnership. Hopefully you too will find it a practical resource as you build an exceptional educational team in your exemplary school.

Chapter 1

Effective School Leadership

There is one single factor common to every educational change initiative, whether it be teacher satisfaction, improved student achievement, or safe and secure schools: the quality of the principal-teacher relationship. When relationships are good and people feel valued and respected, they are willing to go to great lengths to work together to solve the issues that confront them.

The Professional Standards For Educational Leaders, formerly referred to as the standards of the Interstate School Leaders Licensure Consortium (ISLLC), clearly address the need for building relationships as one of the key components of quality schools. As promising as the training that accompanies these standards may be, there is still the immediate need of helping principals deal with the very difficult aspect of facilitating teacher growth and catapulting them to excellence in an environment that is increasingly more demanding and, unfortunately often less and less forgiving.

These standards as well as other federal and state educational initiatives have also heightened the need for administrators to assist teachers in facing student academic achievement and behavioral challenges. While these challenges are often related to teacher skill deficits and/or nonproductive teacher behavior, administrators often report that the tools needed to meet these challenges were not provided in their principal preparation training, as noted in Levine's 2005 study, "Educating School Leaders."

THE PRINCIPAL LEADER

As the leader of the professional teaching staff and the coordinator of a cadre of classified personnel, the principal remains the key to whether a school is considered a pleasant and productive place to work. For decades, principal training has focused on leadership style and theory, and while these are important components of leading a quality school, the glue that holds a school together and allows the leader to deal with the tough issues is the quality of the relationship between the principal and the teacher.

Principals have the ability to improve relationships with teachers by attending to those aspects of the principal-teacher relationship that build trust, collegiality, and commitment. It is the responsibility of the leader to be the consummate relationship builder—encouraging, motivating, and respecting each teacher as the valued person he or she is—as these daily interpersonal interactions are the barometer of what is happening in the school. A principal who is actively involved and clearly visible in the hallways as well as the classrooms, one who is cheerleading the efforts of the teachers, is the one who is actively providing the vision for the school in a positive, proactive manner.

Yet, even when the principal has a positive and encouraging manner, there is one area of the role that many, if not most, do not relish: handling the often difficult teacher issues. The reality is that difficult issues, if ignored, can become like a cancer in the organization, affecting everyone in a manner that becomes toxic to the entire school.

So if this measure of school toxicity is at stake, why do so many principals often ignore these issues until they reach monumental proportions? When queried, many, especially those new to their roles, believe they are inadequately prepared in this area.

One thing to keep in mind is that many teachers' performance problems are related to not only professional development but also personal development. For example, how they deal with change, diversity, or conflict on the personal level often relates to how they execute classroom management and organization, develop positive relationships with students, and encourage student responsibility required for academic success. Our goal is to help you, the principal, address how to handle many of these difficult teacher issues in a way that builds the kind of school the public expects, ultimately creating the kind of environment that not only empowers teachers but is also healthy and whole for all.

A leader's role is never easy. Difficult decisions and situations confront the principal on a daily basis, and it is the school leader's responsibility to consistently make good decisions and to move the school in a positive direction. This can most effectively happen if one maintains the heart of a leader.

THE HEART OF THE LEADER

As previously established, the success of every institution begins with the leader, which in education is the building principal. Whether the principal is successful or not has everything to do with what he or she believes, values, and dreams about, which exemplifies the heart of the leader or that to which he or she is committed. What a person believes deep down in the essence of his or her being and how that belief is played out through visible actions is the determining factor of the person's success as a principal. Teachers and others with whom the principal interacts are motivated by those actions, and in the final analysis, the effectiveness of the school is in large part dependent on them. In fact, if there is a disconnect between the belief system of the principal and the teachers, effectiveness will often be minimized.

Teachers, like students, are quick to intuit the principal's character and his or her commitment to them as individuals. While the organization does not become a caring and productive environment if the leader is self-absorbed or duplicitous, those schools that are great emanate from the individuals'—principals' and teachers'—shared commitment to each other driven by a genuine love for the students they serve.

Regardless of where you stand in the endless debate of whether a leader is born or made, clear characteristics consistently surface in good and effective principals. These characteristics are essential in assisting teachers become successful within a safe, caring, and productive learning environment. Good principals

1. Lead from the **head and the heart**. They think with their hearts as well as their heads. While they abide by the principles of the organization, they balance these responsibilities with care and concern, thereby creating win-win situations.
2. Model **humility,** recognizing their own humanity. They are quick to admit their mistakes and to see others' mistakes as a learning tool. This creates an atmosphere of creativity and risk taking that empowers teachers.
3. Exemplify **trustworthiness**. They can be trusted. It is essential that they are individuals who follow through on what they say, who are not duplicitous, and who will be honest with others even in the most difficult situations. People need to feel that the person to whom they report is someone who will be there for them when the going gets tough.
4. Demonstrate **a heartfelt caring.** They genuinely care for the people with whom they work. They are not only interested in what happens in the classroom and in the building at large, but also interested in the teacher as a person. This extends to their interest in what is happening in the teacher's personal life, not as an intrusive measure but as an expression of their care and concern for the teacher's well-being. The caring principal is ready to step up and assist wherever necessary, even when the teacher has personal or family issues.
5. Offer **genuine encouragement,** quickly focusing on the positive and looking for opportunities to celebrate teacher success. They often reframe situations in such a way that even mistakes or bad decisions are viewed as opportunities to improve. Effective principals recognize that praise does not detract from them but serves to build confidence, competence, and self-esteem of the faculty they serve.
6. Maintain a **sense of perspective.** They have the ability to look at situations not only from their perspective but also from the perspective of others. This sense of perspective increases teacher confidence in them, which often results in the staff being willing to make sacrifices they normally wouldn't make because they know they are listened to and heard.
7. Keep a **sense of humor.** They are quick to laugh at themselves and to see humor in even the darkest of times. They don't take themselves too seriously, and as a result, the staff learns to feel less stressed, creating a culture of optimism.
8. Offer **respect**. They earn the teachers' respect by being respectful. They realize that respect comes not from the position they hold but from how they treat others and how they are perceived.
9. Actively **promote** and help teachers grow and achieve new heights. They actively encourage teachers to seek new opportunities to improve their teaching and to set higher goals for themselves that might even result in them moving to other positions that may be outside the building.
10. Are **loving**. Ultimately, great principals are those who are seen by the teachers as fair and honest, constantly encouraging them to strive for even greater excellence, those who love and care for them.

The best principals are those who build positive and meaningful relationships with teachers, parents, and students and do so in an others-oriented manner. Sometimes this even means knowing when the "fit" of the teacher is not the best for the school or even for the profession. Principals who embrace the thought that their role is to empower and encourage others and who are accountable for their actions are the ones who build the most loyal and forgiving staff and who partner with them in creating an exemplary school.

CHAPTER 1 QUESTIONS TO PONDER

1. If I randomly select five teachers and staff and ask them what characteristics I exemplify as a leader, how would they respond? Do they think I try to work out win-win solutions to issues that arise? Do they feel empowered to creatively seek solutions to problems and become risk takers in doing so? Do they feel assured that even when the going gets tough, I'll be there?
2. When was the last time I expressed an interest in what was happening in the lives of the faculty and staff apart from school?
3. When was the last time I was vulnerable and actually laughed at myself?
4. Do I routinely promote and encourage the teachers in my care to seek new opportunities to improve?
5. In reflecting upon my day today, have I been fair and honest in my interactions with others?
6. What can I do to more visibly show that I have the heart of a leader?

Chapter 2

Establishing an Open, Caring, and Positive School Climate and Culture

The heart of the leader exhibited through positive and meaningful relationships generally results *in* and is the result *of* an open, caring, and positive school climate and culture. Even in this generally positive environment, one must face the realities that each day principals are faced with a multitude of opportunities and challenges, and while each is different, some situations are recurrent. With those, it is important for school leaders to know how they will generally respond. In other words, having a general plan of action for everyday occurrences goes a long way in creating and maintaining a quality school.

If every situation is handled as though it is a new and unexpected event, chances are a principal will soon be overwhelmed by the mundane and not be prepared to handle the really significant situations that do happen. Instead, beginning with a general plan for the everyday challenges and then adapting and adjusting that plan as required to reach a principled solution, gives a supervisor a leg up and provides him or her the opportunity for taking immediate decisive action. Being able to move quickly with confidence gives the faculty and staff a sense of security knowing their leader is in charge and able to handle whatever situation arises. This confidence sets a positive tone while creating a sense of safety and security that carries through to every aspect of the environment. It also prevents everyday situations from snowballing into major incidents that can easily destabilize a school.

To provide insights into ongoing general trials that often plague an organization on a regular basis, we offer in this chapter some useful understandings around 15 of these issues as well as some guidelines into how they can be handled. While not an exhaustive list by any means, it is intended to provide a broad range of issues a school leader may confront and to provide him or her with sufficient information to develop a repertoire of responses that can serve as an initial base for responding. These strategies can be adjusted and adapted to meet the needs of specific situations and to provide a basis for further planning. We address the following general challenges that if handled correctly can be used to facilitate an open and caring culture:

BUILDING CREDIBILITY

There is probably no one aspect of leadership that matters more than being credible. Unfortunately credibility is not something you can speak into existence. Instead, it is something that is built over time. People want to be able to trust their principal, but in order for that to occur, you have to be worthy of belief and confidence. Credibility is built by being consistent and faithful to the charge you have as a leader and having the integrity to stand strong in the face of criticism or challenge.

Useful Understandings:

1. Credibility is important if you expect people to take risks and to make the commitment to go the extra mile in order to better the organization.
2. Credibility is built by actions, not words, and can quickly be destroyed when these are not consistently aligned.
3. Credibility begins with a willingness to admit your mistakes.

Guidelines:

1. Be sure when you say you are going to do something that you can in fact make it happen, and if it is questionable, be willing to admit that you are going to try to do something but you don't know for sure that you can make it happen.
2. Be willing to stand up for the faculty and staff and protect them in the face of attacks or criticism.
3. Be willing to discuss any issue as long as it doesn't break confidentiality.
4. Demonstrate that you are putting the needs of others first.
5. Don't over promise.
6. Consider questions and interruptions as opportunities for open dialogue.
7. Be candid when asked a question, even if you are uncomfortable.

8. Communicate, communicate, communicate. People begin to lose trust when rumors are never dealt with or when there are major changes occurring they don't know about.

COMBATING EXCUSES

Excuses are generally explanations of our actions designed to minimize their negative implications and to help maintain a positive image of ourselves. We tend to make excuses when we fear condemnation or recrimination for something we have done or failed to do. When excuses become a normal response, it is very detrimental to both the person and the organization.

Useful Understandings:

1. People are less likely to defend themselves with excuses in an atmosphere that is supportive and noncondemning concerning failure and mistakes.
2. Leaders who never acknowledge their own mistakes or shortcomings tend to reinforce excuse-making because they create an unforgiving atmosphere.

Guidelines:

1. Encourage confession of mistakes by example.
2. Remain nonjudgmental when hearing what sounds like an excuse because the person may really have a valid reason for doing or not doing what you had desired.
3. Attempt to understand the root of the excuse-making rather than just the symptom if you want to make real changes in the person's behavior.
4. Use praise and affirmation often. Employees who are secure in their positions and themselves are less likely to make excuses.
5. Make sure employee expectations are realistic if you want to avoid unnecessary excuses.
6. Before taking any action, try to understand why people tend to be making excuses.
7. Focus on fixing the problem and not on blaming. Over time, this serves to exponentially reduce excuse-making.

COMBATING RUMORS

Rumors are the bane of every organization. The more people feel left out of what is happening, the more they tend to engage in rumor mongering. Rumors cannot be eliminated, but they can be curtailed significantly depending on how they are handled.

Useful Understandings:

1. An organization that has fear, has poor communication, has limited skills, or lacks a clear vision lends itself to rumors.

2. Rumors start when there is a need for communication and it is not forthcoming. In those situations, facts are combined with individual perception and sold as truth.
3. Information is power, and when employees have information that will advance their status, they easily fall prey to sharing information that often is only partially true.
4. Sometimes rumor-spreading or gossip-sharing are the vehicles used to get revenge, and in the social media era, this damaging information can go viral almost instantaneously.

Guidelines:

1. Curtail rumors by providing employees with as much information about any action or plan that is being considered as is humanly or legally possible.
2. Establish a culture in the organization of appropriate silence regarding confidential issues and reinforce it regularly, taking necessary steps when confidentiality has been broken.
3. Address the issue at hand and immediately share as much as possible when rumors begin.
4. Encourage people to ask questions without fear and make yourself open to answering any question that is legitimate.
5. Develop mechanisms so that people know how to get their questions answered.
6. Schedule meetings to address issues surrounding gossip.
7. Choose a person to serve as a mediator to deal with gossip or the rumor in question when they are of a personal nature.

CORRECTIVE ACTION FOR RESULTS

The need for corrective action is something that occurs yet is often done haphazardly, resulting in an environment that eats away at the very fabric of the organization. When attention to discipline is avoided by the administrator, problems tend to mount, and then when discipline is used, it becomes far too punitive and does not result in positive change. Learning the best timing for when to correct is as important for a principal to know as understanding the purpose and nature of the discipline.

Useful Understandings:

1. Good leaders create a productive working environment in which the enforcement of rules and procedures is a natural process because everyone knows, understands, and accepts the expectations.
2. Disciplining someone through punitive measures alone does not enhance job performance or foster loyalty or commitment. Instead, it often breeds resentment further impairing job productivity.
3. Discipline can be most beneficial when one has the opportunity to collaboratively engage in problem-solving with the supervisor and when they mutually agree upon a plan to change the behavior.

4. Supervisors need to intervene in developing issues rather than waiting until there is an incident that requires more formal efforts. This can only happen successfully when a good relationship has been established.

Guidelines:

1. Identify the underlying cause for actions that require supervisory intervention.
2. Make sure you deal with facts and not innuendoes or rumors.
3. Discuss the problem in a nonthreatening manner with the attitude of trying to understand the core issue.
4. Problem solve with the employee, looking for a way to address the issue and to ultimately change the behavior.
5. Make sure clear expectations have been discussed before closing the meeting.
6. Utilize facts when helping the employee understand organizational policies and procedures regarding the type of incident being discussed.
7. Actively listen in order to maximize the chance that you will be successful in overcoming resistance.
8. Be prepared to offer whatever it takes for the person to get back on the right track, which may include coaching, mentoring, or even special adaptations.
9. Help the individual understand the need to assume personal responsibility for his or her issues or behaviors and that there is a need for change but if he or she does not, then be ready to take more formal means of changing the behavior.
10. Understand the general course of disciplinary efforts for your organization:
    a. Facilitate an oral discussion in an informal setting where the problem can be openly addressed.
    b. Follow up with a written memo laying out the problem that needs to be addressed and the plan of action.
    c. Place the individual on probation for failing to live up to the written memo.
    d. Suspend the individual.
    e. Terminate if necessary, but be sure to exhaust all corrective actions before formally terminating an individual.

DEALING WITH CRISES

Crises occur in any organization, and even though you cannot plan for them, there are some commonsense strategies that you can use to not only avert them but also deal with them when they do occur. It seems that crises occur most often when there is a loss of something important or of value. It can be a tangible thing such as an unexpected conflict with a student, parent, or another employee, or it could be something that is perceived to threaten another's status or position. Whatever the cause, a crisis is generally a situation where a person's normal coping abilities or methods seem to not work and a new and different approach needs to be found in order to end it.

Useful Understandings:

1. Crises are pivotal points that bring opportunities for positive change and growth.
2. If the staff does not realize the importance of ongoing two-way interaction, they may interpret this as uncertainty or indecisiveness and it may increase the likelihood of confusion.
3. Make sure in a crisis that you have people with the technical skills to maintain a productive dialogue with each other and who have sufficient time for consultation.
4. If staff are unable to be productive during a crisis, then you as the leader must exercise your position power and move forward to solve it, but even in this mode, be sure to involve as many people as necessary and communicate with all involved.
5. During a crisis, often you have to make split-second decisions. Still with a posture of maintaining effective two-way communication, revisit those decisions with the staff post-crisis.

Guidelines:

1. Prioritize what needs to be done during a crisis so that you don't go down a meaningless rabbit trail.
2. Over communicate with faculty and staff so they know what is happening and reassure them at every opportunity.
3. Keep focused on what needs to be done and avoid extraneous issues that can be dealt with later.
4. Stay in charge during a crisis in a manner that is supportive. People are looking for leadership they can trust, but they don't want to be left out.
5. Be sure you are present during the time of crisis or if not, be sure that you have trained someone to take the lead in your absence. People need to know that someone of authority is on site, on the scene, and involved in discussions.
6. Be prepared to fall on your sword if necessary. No one is willing to follow a leader who begins to double talk or disperses false information in order to avoid blame. It is critical that you take responsibility.
7. When the crisis is over, make sure you draw people together to discuss what happened, what worked, and how it could have been handled better. This will make the faculty and staff more comfortable in future situations that may be ambiguous and possibly lead to crisis.

HOW TO CONTEND WITH JOB PRESSURE

At one time or another, all of us feel pressure that can either be motivating or debilitating. As a principal, it is critical that you pick up on the cues when someone is beginning to feel too much stress, and before it becomes a real issue, step in and provide assistance in helping the individual begin to successfully navigate through it.

Useful Understandings:

1. Stress is the price of attempting to adapt to the demands of the environment.

2. As a reaction to something in the environment, stress causes some type of effect. Its true source is our interpretation or perception of the situation: what it means to us.

3. Stress can be positive when it stimulates motivation and achievement, while allowing the individual to perform at a peak level. It can also be harmful depending on how the individual perceives the situation.

4. Signs of stress most often noticed are typically either physical or psychological. You may notice increased absenteeism due to a myriad of medical issues such as headaches, digestive disorders, or insurmountable fatigue triggered by insomnia, which may or may not be caused by anger, depression, or anxiety. Within the workplace itself, you may notice such things as moodiness, apathy, and even phobias that are totally uncharacteristic of the individual.

Guidelines:

1. Recognize when a person is stressed and attempt to determine the cause.

2. Evaluate your expectations of the individual and determine if they are realistic or if perhaps you are creating the stress.

3. Be supportive and look for ways to encourage the person.

4. Encourage the employee to determine what they think is the cause of their stress. It may be personal and not work related at all, but merely manifests itself at work.

5. Have the employee evaluate his or her personal expectations and determine if he or she is realistic.

6. Determine if there are practical steps you can take that would help alleviate the stress such as adjusting schedules or rearranging work priorities.

7. Collaboratively establish a concrete plan to help handle the source of the stress and make sure you follow up and maintain necessary contact with the individual.

8. Help the person take one day at a time and keep the issues in proper perspective so they don't become magnified in his or her mind.

9. Encourage the individual to take personal time and find ways to have fun.

HOW TO DETERMINE FACULTY AND STAFF NEEDS

Assessing faculty and staff needs from a proactive approach is an ongoing responsibility of school leaders. Too often needs do not surface until situations become serious and morale is affected. Part of a supervisor's role is to continually assess the needs of the faculty and staff and to provide the necessary leadership and direction to let people know that you are not only aware of their needs, but that you take them seriously.

Useful Understandings:

1. Assessing faculty and staff needs is a way of showing commitment and love, which serves to motivate and give them a sense of being appreciated.

2. Understanding the knowledge, skills, and abilities of the faculty and staff is essential in determining their needs.

3. In order for real needs to surface, it is imperative that there is a sense the workplace is a safe and nonthreatening environment for self-disclosure.
4. Active listening is key. It is not enough just to allow people to speak out; they must feel they have been listened to. The more people feel they are listened to and have a participating role in running the organization, the more needs will surface and the more they will do so early as opposed to later when they can become more unwieldy.
5. As we meet the unsatisfied needs of the faculty and staff, we must keep the goals of the organization in the forefront of our decisions.

Guidelines:

1. Set aside regular formal and informal times to focus on assessing needs.
2. Attempt, to the degree possible, to meet the emotional needs of faculty and staff as it is the bellwether of whether meeting other needs will be sufficient.
3. Advocate ongoing training as it builds skill, increases confidence, and shapes esprit de corps within the organization.
4. Maintain attitude and actions that send the clear message that your job is to give faculty and staff the proper support and training necessary to ensure they will be the best they can be in the jobs they hold.
5. Listen actively.
6. Establish a prevailing level of trust, commitment, and honesty so you and your employees can collaboratively identify needs and solve problems during key times such as performance appraisals.

HOW TO HANDLE COMPLAINTS

Complaints are a reality in any organization or relationship. The tone and basis for them can be key to understanding whether they are toxic or if they are simply a way of asking for a little attention. We all prefer to not hear complaints, but handled appropriately they can become an excellent tool for gauging the health of the organization, much like the canaries were for determining if the gases in the mine were at a dangerous level.

Useful Understandings:

1. Complaining may be some people's way of receiving the attention they feel they can only get in this manner.
2. Complaints can be handled formally or informally depending on their nature.
3. Complaints from an individual employee may be a reflection of a larger number of people but this person is the only one willing to voice discontent.
4. Complaints may contain valid suggestions while cloaked in defensive or even offensive language.
5. Complaints should be taken seriously and attended to even if you think they are meaningless.

6. Providing an effective mechanism for dealing with concerns will minimize complaining that is detrimental and toxic to morale.

Guidelines:

1. Maintain an open communication pipeline that encourages faculty and staff to come to you with concerns.
2. Be punctual in dealing with employees' concerns or complaints. Allowing too much time to pass before doing so creates cynicism on the part of faculty and staff, lowering morale.
3. Handle complaints in a private and individual manner not only to protect privacy but to keep matters under control.
4. Avoid being defensive. When listening to complaints, try to restate the concern so that you understand it as well as its driving motivation. Do not argue as that only sends the message that nothing will happen.
5. Make sure you know what the person wants to happen with the complaint and then act accordingly in relation to its validity, type, and seriousness. Sometimes people just want to be heard and don't want to have any action taken.
6. Make sure that individuals involved in a complaint walk away feeling respected and affirmed even if the matter did not turn out as they had expected.

HOW TO LEARN FROM MISTAKES

Mistakes are a fact of life. Everyone makes them, but unfortunately too often we don't learn from our errors. Instead, we repeat them and in doing so we begin to lose the confidence of those around us. Today, it seems people make mistakes and, too often, rather than owning them with personal accountability, they attempt to blame someone else. On the other hand, a successful leader not only accepts responsibility for his or her mistakes but attempts to learn from them.

Useful Understandings:

1. Mistakes happen to everyone and should be seen as learning and/or teaching opportunities.
2. When people feel free to take risks, the chance of mistakes occurs proportionately, yet the environment that promotes risk taking ultimately leads to greater success.
3. Mistakes can be turned into a positive experience, if handled correctly.

Guidelines:

1. Admit your mistakes. Rather than losing credibility, people tend to respect more a leader who not only admits that he or she made a mistake but openly accepts responsibility for it.
2. Realize that all mistakes are not equal. Some are serious and will call for analysis and corrective action; however, mistakes that cause no harm to the organization or the people are learning opportunities.

3. Analyze your mistakes. If they are a reoccurring problem, they need to be examined for their cause. Oftentimes mistakes are simply the results of carelessness or inattentiveness, but they can also be an indication of a more serious character issue.
4. If you make a mistake, be open and upfront about it, and, if necessary, apologize to whoever is affected by it. This builds trust and openness in the organization. Don't continue to blame yourself or others for an error. Move on. Try to resolve the reason for a mistake and change what is being done to cause it. Once you have done what is necessary to deal with the fallout from a mistake, shut the door on it and don't rehash it over and over. Not only is this unhealthy, but it also lessens your leadership effectiveness.

HOW TO LISTEN EFFECTIVELY

We all like to think we listen effectively, but in truth most of us do not. We are busy thinking about what we are going to say next or thinking of ways we can rebut what the other person just told us. Listening effectively is an absolute must for any school leader's success. It takes patience and forbearance to allow someone to finish speaking when you feel they have misunderstood or they are in the wrong, but allowing someone to finish their comments before responding does wonders for relationships.

Useful Understandings:

1. Most people only truly hear 5–15% of what is spoken. Without a complete exchange of information, there is no suitable basis for action.
2. A person is a good listener when he or she shuts out distractions, asks direct questions, rephrases, doesn't fake understanding, grasps themes rather than memorizes the details, puts aside his or her own desire to talk, and gives minimal encouragers as others speak.
3. Active listening facilitates all aspects of a relationship and helps people know they are valued.
4. Bad listening habits include faking attention, criticizing the tone, listening selectively, breaking eye contact, and interrupting.

Guidelines:

1. Listen actively.
2. Recognize listening as a skill and practice it. Develop positive listening responses such as eye contact, attentive body language, reflecting feeling, paraphrasing, and clarifying.
3. Use open-ended questions to encourage more in-depth responses.
4. Be aware of emotional responses that may get in the way of the facts or issues. Your goal is to focus and refocus on the facts.
5. Find common agreement before disagreeing.
6. Put aside your preconceived notions.
7. Avoid making value judgments.

8. Learn the receiver's preferred communication style and speak to him or her in a way that will be heard.

HOW TO RUN A GOOD MEETING

Nothing can drain more energy or deplete a happy mood quicker than being in an unproductive meeting. In today's world, meetings, which can be either draining or incredibly productive, seem to be a major part of everyone's schedule. Having a specific and reasonable agenda before you go into a meeting can almost guarantee it will be profitable to everyone involved.

Useful Understandings:

1. Make sure you begin and end meetings on time, because if you start late, you will find that even on-time people will also begin to arrive late.
2. If you are going to run overtime in a meeting, it is a good idea to suggest that if those involved could stay for just another 10 minutes, you can complete the business at hand and avoid the need for another meeting. That lets people know there is an end in sight and most of them are willing to hang in there with you.
3. People tend to need a bit of a warm up in which they catch up with what is happening in the lives of those who are in attendance. It sets a kind of family atmosphere and allows people the time to prepare themselves for the meeting. Just make sure it doesn't go too long.
4. In every meeting you will find people who have ideas or thoughts and unless you draw them out, you will never hear what they have to say. Make sure you identify those people and when appropriate solicit their thoughts.

Guidelines:

1. Provide the agenda in advance whenever possible as this allows those in attendance to prepare and to bring other materials they think might be valuable.
2. Keep the meeting as brief as possible. As chair, it is your responsibility to stay focused, keep the meeting moving along, and ensure that peripheral issues don't take over the agenda.
3. Allow for breaks if you anticipate a long meeting. People often need to catch up on other issues in their offices or use the facilities. If you do this, you will have fewer people getting up to leave the room during the meeting. It also keeps the time together focused.
4. Share the credit for any successes your meeting group has. If there is someone who has accomplished something special, acknowledge them. This builds group cohesiveness.
5. Don't make people feel small by putting them down or by making them look bad in front of others.
6. Inject humor into your meeting. This keeps the mood light and maintains a more cooperative atmosphere.

7. Avoid addressing personal issues during a meeting. This is not the place to settle them, much less is it the place to ignite emotions by belittling or embarrassing someone.

MOTIVATING FOR SUCCESS

Motivating people is a must in any organization. Much literature tells us what it takes to motivate someone, but even then, it is still somewhat of an intangible. What motivates one person doesn't necessarily motivate another, because, as we know, personal circumstances directly affect one's outlook. We also know that how a person feels about his or her job has a direct effect on their motivation. The key for the school leader is to understand a person's desires, strengths, and particular talents and to assess what needs to happen in order for a person to be motivated and to do what is necessary.

Useful Understandings:

1. Behavior is goal directed, success oriented, and responsive to rewards. If you are to be successful in motivating, you need to be attentive to an employee's personal, self-motivated goals, and his or her motivations for attaining those goals.
2. Variables contributing to high motivation are morale, job satisfaction, supervision practices, group cohesion, recognition, responsibility, and advancement opportunities.
3. Establishing personal relationships with faculty and staff is essential to building motivation.
4. Focusing on an employee's strengths tends to encourage a positive attitude and promotes a motivating environment.

Guidelines:

1. Provide a safe and secure environment that encourages risk taking without reprisal.
2. Place employees in positions that utilize their strengths. This builds confidence.
3. Maximize the potential for motivating by
   a. Identifying employees' strengths,
   b. Encouraging creativity and new ideas,
   c. Providing a supportive environment,
   d. Affirming the employee's efforts,
   e. Providing supervision on an as-needed basis focusing on coming alongside rather than on evaluation,
   f. Making sure expectations and procedures are well known in order to provide structure and to avoid ambiguity which can quickly become a demotivator, and
   g. Creating a means for productive input, decision making, and problem-solving. Employees who are affirmed and accepted become committed and motivated.

PLANNING EFFECTIVELY

Planning ahead is critical in leading a school. Too often, planning is paid lip service, and once plans are developed, they are seldom looked at because the tyranny of the immediate seems to take all of the time. Ultimately without proper planning, the organization takes on a chaotic sense that begins to undermine staff morale and leaves a lot of uncertainty as to where the organization is going. Good planning goes a long way in preventing that. While planning is a process that provides direction to an organization, it is not immutable. Good plans are subject to changes and revisions simply because that is the nature of the educational process. There are, however, things that can be done to plan effectively.

Useful Understandings:

1. Good planning is focused and goal oriented.
2. While long-term goals are generally aspirations, short-term goals need to be specific and doable.
3. Good planning involves all of the people affected by the plan, thus encouraging buy in.
4. Good planning is flexible planning.
5. Planning must lead to measurable outcomes.
6. Remember, there is a high correlation between good planning and high productivity.

Guidelines:

1. Take into consideration the strengths and weaknesses of the faculty and staff.
2. Answer key questions while in the planning process (e.g., Do we have the proper expertise to achieve our goals? What training and support will be needed? Do we have the resources needed to complete the plan?)
3. Delegate appropriately and don't over depend on one individual.
4. Make sure everyone has a role in carrying out the plan.
5. Follow through on whatever you plan.
6. Monitor progress regularly, and if a change is required, involve the group again to make the necessary adjustments.

PROMOTING CHANGE

Change is something we all talk about, but not many of us embrace. Many people fear change since it often upsets what we have been doing and leaves us feeling somewhat insecure. Creating productive and sustainable organizational change requires buy in from those involved.

Useful Understandings:

1. Change only occurs when people feel there is a need to change.

2. Change often makes people uncomfortable and unwilling to risk.
3. People need a role model when considering change; otherwise it becomes frightening.
4. There is a prevailing fear among people when making a change, that it will not be successful and they may be held responsible.
5. For change to occur, people want to know that things will be better than before and that it is personally advantageous.

Guidelines:

1. Decide exactly what change you want to occur and be sure you can explain clearly why the change is necessary.
2. Talk about the success of other organizations that have made similar changes.
3. Be prepared to sell the vision of change.
4. Identify people in the organization who are excellent change agents and get them involved in serving as leaders overseeing and monitoring its success.
5. Celebrate the successes of change frequently and take time to encourage and support those who are having difficulty.
6. Be prepared to make modifications if certain aspects of the change need some tweaking. Don't buy into your change to the degree that there is no room for improvement.
7. Encourage assessment of the change and its process with the idea of how we can improve what we are doing, not who is to blame for any failures that occur.

RECEIVING STAFF COOPERATION

Getting staff to cooperate with administrators is another key to supervisory success. Position allows leaders to order something done but without a willingness on the part of employees to actively participate, cooperation is minimal.

Useful Understandings:

1. Small cohesive groups make for a greater sense of community than large impersonal groups.
2. A feeling of membership is a must if cooperation is to be achieved.
3. Characteristics of a cooperative group are cohesion, honesty, acceptance, responsibility, and trust.
4. Competitiveness is reduced when staff members feel secure and understand the value of their function.
5. Research has shown that a high percentage of employees are suspicious of other people's motives and do not trust easily, so building trust goes a long way toward getting cooperation.

Guidelines:

1. Ensure that goals and objectives are clear in order that a common starting point can be obtained. The clearer the expectations and understanding become, the greater the cooperation.
2. Ensure that lines of communication are open in such a way that faculty and staff feel they and their ideas are being respected.
3. Be open and interested in exchanges between yourself and employees. The more vulnerable you make yourself, the greater the trust.
4. Recognize and appreciate the group norm of the organization, as your goal is to create a cohesive group. Whenever possible get people to work in small groups where they can build familiarity, openness, and trust. As a small group, they become more proactive and are more free to speak up.
5. Encourage collaboration not only to equip faculty and staff, but also to give them roles of significance in the organizational operation.
6. Involve faculty and staff whenever possible. The more ownership they sense, the more likely they are to cooperate in a positive and significant way no matter how difficult the task.

While it is important to establish a positive climate and culture, it is also important to understand that none of us comes to school every day functioning at the highest level of emotional maturity. There are some days that because of personal, health, or emotional reasons, we operate at a pretty low stage of motivation. For some, the general disposition might very well be self-absorbed or approval oriented which inhibits and often interferes with the ability to contribute in the most positive way. At other times, and hopefully most times, we are more relationship or, better yet, others oriented. The next chapter focuses on the four stages of motivational development, which all of us pass through on the way to developing a strong sense of self-efficacy.

CHAPTER 2 QUESTIONS TO PONDER

1. Do I move quickly and confidently providing the faculty and staff a sense that I can handle whatever situation arises, while maintaining the heart of a leader?
2. What do I do to exemplify credibility within the building?
3. What do I do to facilitate an environment that is supportive and nonthreatening?
4. When was the last time I acknowledged a personal failure or mistake?
5. If I randomly selected five teachers and staff, would they say I lead by fear and intimidation or by encouragement and empowerment?

Chapter 3

Four Stages of Motivational Development

While displaying the heart of a leader, exemplary principals are keenly aware that most quality teachers don't just suddenly materialize; they pass through various stages of motivation as they grow and mature throughout their professional careers. The goal of the effective leader is to recognize these various stages in an effort to assist teachers move to the next higher level as they continue to strive for professional competence and exemplary performance.

As you explore these four stages, it is critical to remember that individual behavior is highly contextual. It is also critical to remember to never put anyone in a box. Just because they may act at stage one in one area doesn't necessarily mean he or she may act that way in all situations. It also doesn't mean they can't change at the drop of a hat. Instead, these stages merely give us a starting point from which to begin in our goal of improving teacher performance.

FOUR STAGES OF MOTIVATION

Adapted from Hersey and Blanchard (1982) and Selig and Arroyo (1989), the *Four Stages of Motivation* (see Textbox 3.1) provides a framework and an umbrella for examining teacher competence and self-efficacy.

At each level, a person makes a decision based on certain needs and his or her desires, sense of worth, confidence, and circumstances that arise. Generally we operate at one of the four stages, but sometimes we reach a new stage or even sometime slip to a lower level based on what is happening in our lives. The way we perceive the

Textbox 3.1 **Four Stages of Motivation**

Stage 1: Self-Absorbed
Stage 2: Approval Oriented
Stage 3: Relationship Oriented
Stage 4: Others Oriented

world has a lot to do with what stage of motivation we reach. It is hoped that over time all of us would be striving to reach stage four but in reality, that is not always the case.

As a principal you will have teachers at a variety of levels. One of your jobs is to work with these teachers to help them grow in their stage of motivation, because, as they grow, the better teacher they will become, the greater role they will play in building a productive and pace-setting school.

It is also necessary to look at yourself as a principal and ask yourself regularly, "Am I acting at the highest stage of motivation possible?" The lower your stage of development, the lower the teacher's general stage of development will tend to be since, in large part, you play a major role in determining the general level of motivation of your school.

The more you understand the stages of motivation, the better you will be at determining how best to interact and communicate with individual teachers. It is your role to encourage and counsel in a manner that will contribute to teachers' growth.

Stage One: Self-Absorbed

Teachers at this stage, more often than not, are self-absorbed and need direct supervision and specific instruction in order to perform successfully. Often due to a lack of professional competency or its often accompanying self-efficacy issues, individuals functioning at this level are motivated by a need to survive. They tend to feel a lack of confidence in their ability to perform successfully so they need opportunities to master the basic routine tasks of the profession. Because this is a low-level stage of development, principals may experience passive-aggressive behavior or even outright hostility as they work with these individuals, particularly if it is an issue of self-efficacy.

Stage Two: Approval Oriented

Driven by a need for approval, teachers at this stage tend to require less direct supervision as they demonstrate a better grasp of essential teaching skills. While often displaying a lack of confidence because they may be overwhelmed by the multitude of decisions required of them as a teacher, they are more able to assume responsibility for defined projects within the school. With encouragement, they increasingly demonstrate more willingness to attempt new teaching approaches or complex learning projects and they are much more willing to engage with other teachers in shared projects and activities.

Stage Three: Relationship Oriented

Focusing on relationships, teaching skill is demonstrably better due to an increased confidence level in the ability to stimulate students through knowledge and ideas. Teachers at this stage also are in the process of building close working relationships with their colleagues. They relish sharing ideas and often engage less proficient teachers by quickly offering assistance and encouragement. They have a clear idea of the processes involved in teaching and are excellent in promoting teacher-parent relationships.

Stage Four: Others Oriented

Teachers at this stage operate fairly independently. They not only perform admirably in the classroom, but also provide direction to the larger organization. They are truly teacher leaders and are able to adapt to almost any situation. They are confident, perseverant, and extremely competent.

MOTIVATING FORCES, MOTIVATION INDICATORS, AND IDENTIFYING BEHAVIORAL CHARACTERISTICS OF THE FOUR STAGES

Maintaining an awareness of the motivating forces, motivation indicators, and the identifying behavioral characteristics of those at the various stages of motivation (see Table 3.1) enable principals to use the appropriate supervisory style to meet the needs of the individual and to assist him or her in moving to the next stage of growth. By addressing those needs, then you, as a principal, can help teachers gain confidence to continue in their development; however, if a teacher's needs at a certain stage are not met, there is little chance he or she will develop the tools necessary for further growth.

Oftentimes difficulties in teacher performance are simply a matter of professional competence, and in those cases, they can be easily remedied with quality supervision and training. However, more often than not, a teacher's stage of professional competence relates to the person's level of self-efficacy and reflects a particular stage of motivation.

Let's look at a practical example. As a principal, you may want teachers to demonstrate more flexibility in lesson planning. Your first strategy is to work with them to develop confidence in the skills they already possess and encourage them to take more risks in planning and implementation. Teachers at Stage 3 or 4 will more than likely not only accomplish this goal but also thrive as they take the necessary steps to do so. On the other hand, it is likely that teachers at Stage 1 or 2 will have difficulty because they lack confidence in their competence and, therefore, risk taking may result in them, losing what little security they do possess. If you provide a significant amount of structure, most teachers will begin to attempt some risk taking, even if they do so cautiously. The more protected and safe they feel as they do something new, the more likely they will be to take the next steps as their confidence increases.

Although teachers typically demonstrate the characteristics of one or possibly two general stages, that level may fluctuate depending on the stressors that are active in their lives at the time. In other words, teachers may demonstrate different stages of growth depending not only on their competence levels but also on a host of environmental factors, the difficulty of the task, or even more noticeably, their stress level. Some of those stressors may be external to the school and some may be occurring within the school itself. As a principal, if one is to lead from both the head and the heart, it is imperative to be cognizant that these influences often determine the teacher's current stage. With that in mind, you then need to focus on the critical quality issues and provide the kind of supervisory intervention necessary to encourage professional growth as noted in Table 3.2.

Now that you are more familiar with the four Stages of Motivation, we encourage you to self-reflect before you begin to assess the behavior or attitudes of others. Once you have determined the Stage of Motivation, you can move to the next phase, looking at Behavior Style.

CHAPTER 3 QUESTIONS TO PONDER

1. In self-reflection, at what stage do I see my professional behavior and attitude? Which characteristics exemplify this?
2. Am I acting at the highest stage of motivation possible and if not, what can I change to do so?
3. What circumstances cause me to slip from one stage of motivation to another?
4. How am I sensitive to both the internal and the external stressors in the lives of others?
5. Do I feel confident in my ability to appropriately assess others without any type of judgmental attitude?

Table 3.1   Stages of Motivation and Behavioral Characteristics

	Stage 1 *Self-Absorbed*	Stage 2 *Approval Oriented*	Stage 3 *Relationship Oriented*	Stage 4 *Others Oriented*
Motivating Forces	• Autonomy • Fulfillment of basic survival needs • Security • Self-gratification • Self-protection	• Acceptance • Approval • Belonging • Prestige • Recognition	• Affiliation and relationships • Belonging • Competence • Respect • Responsibility	• Equity • Flexibility • Goals • Justice • Meeting the needs of others • Peace • Truth
Motivation Indicators	• External locus of control • Lack of flexibility • Low responsiveness • Limited purpose	• Developing problem-solving skills • Growing adaptability • Mixed external/internal locus of control • Sense of humor	• Abstract thinking • Caring • Goal directed • Healthy expectations • Internal locus of control	• Adaptability • Autonomy • Empathy • Hardy belief in future • Reflection planning skills • Sense of power • Strong internal locus of control
Identifying Behavioral Characteristics	• Tends to view life from the perspective of how it will benefit me • Can become obstinate or passive-aggressive when opposed or frustrated • Quick to complain about people and practices • Responds to verbal praise but is suspicious of others' motives • Functions best when expectations are clear	• Continues to please self but does so by gaining approval of others • Acquiesces to authority quickly even when not in agreement • Seeks opportunity to be in the spotlight • Responds quickly to verbal praise • Performs well with constant guidance	• Looks for ways to contribute to the good of the organization • Able to rethink a position when better alternatives are presented • Tends to seek approval for competence and achievement • Praises others quickly for their efforts • Very much a self-starter	• Sacrifices personal needs for the good of the organization • Can push a point of view while recognizing the merit in opposing arguments • Sees self as a partner in the work of the organization • Has internalized sense of values and is not dependent on others for affirmation • Works well independently

(cont.)

Table 3.1   Stages of Motivation and Behavioral Characteristics (Cont.)

	Stage 1 Self-Absorbed	Stage 2 Approval Oriented	Stage 3 Relationship Oriented	Stage 4 Others Oriented
Identifying Behavioral Characteristics	• Tends toward immediate pay offs for efforts	• Needs to feel part of the group and may quickly regress to Stage 1 if feeling left out	• Sets high standards	• Tends to display confidence while engaging in independent projects
	• Has difficulty accepting authority	• Often directs conversation toward self to gain approval	• Recognizes the needs of others even when it conflicts with their own	• Can discuss any issue in an objective manner without personalizing
	• Often views disagreements as personal attacks	• Poses as a martyr and can be resentful when challenged	• Accepts criticism without personalizing	• Quick to accept guidance and criticism
	• Is concerned about fairness and tends to assess rules from the perspective of how it affects them as opposed to an institutional perspective	• May fake compliance and interest to gain approval	• Very accepting of rules and responsibilities	• Wants to be involved in rule making if possible
	• Has difficulty controlling impulses and often has the mantra for life: "if it feels good do it."	• Likes to express individuality in views and appearance if it gains the approval of others	• Tends to be tolerant of differences in people and their style	• Practices what is preached (models well)
	• Has unrealistic assessment of their skills and competence (usually too high)	• May overplay significance of own contributions in order to gain approval	• Works deliberately	• Sets appropriate goals and works to achieve highest potential
	• Avoids taking responsibility for mistakes, often shifting the blame to others	• In taking responsibility, wrestles with conformity versus individuality	• Very diligent and fulfills responsibilities	• Accepts responsibility especially for mistakes
	• Has limited dependability	• Choices are made based upon the approval received	• Willing to make hard choices for the good of the whole group	• Can be depended on to do what is right
	• Easily becomes jealous or envious of others	• Tends to get embarrassed easily if approval not quickly forthcoming	• Very loyal to certain groups	• Accepts criticism of work and adapts accordingly
	• Looks for opportunities to gain advantages for self	• Can be overly critical of self	• Can be occasionally critical and judgmental of others' performance if it negatively affects "the team"	• Motivates others to do well

Identifying Behavioral Characteristics			
• Easily becomes jealous or envious of others	• Tends to get embarrassed easily if approval not quickly forthcoming	• Very loyal to certain groups	• Accepts criticism of work and adapts accordingly
• Looks for opportunities to gain advantages for self	• Can be overly critical of self	• Can be occasionally critical and judgmental of others' performance if it negatively affects "the team"	• Motivates others to do well
• Tends to be pessimistic and untrusting of others	• Tends to have a low level of trust	• Tends to trust others	• Forgives easily and encourages trust
• May be resistant to learning new things	• Is open to learning and growing when given attention	• Is open to learning to increase competence	• Generalizes learning and appropriately applies it to new issues
• In stressful situations will act on their desire to do things their way	• Will withdraw or become aggressive as opinions are challenged	• Makes judgments based on facts	• Very flexible and rational
• Is suspicious of authority	• Will accept mild criticism if it comes from an authority figure	• Can take the roles of others and "feel their pain"	• Encourages others to consider others' opinions or roles
• Lacks flexibility and does not easily see the need to comply with policies or rules	• Will comply with policies and rules but will seek approval when doing so	• Accepts policies and rules and sees them as reasonable and necessary for the good of the organization	• Explains to others about the need to comply, accept, and even own the policies and rules of the organization
• May lack the necessary skills of the position and resists training	• Will accept training if significant approval is given by an authority figure, preferably the principal	• Views professional development and training to be good for the school	• Actively and enthusiastically participates or even leads professional development activities
• Has difficulty accepting the opinions of others	• Will accept opinions of others if approval is needed from them	• Will accept different opinions and weigh them objectively.	• Seeks out different opinions to understand all sides of an issue
• Has difficulty generalizing	• Makes limited generalizations	• Able to make fairly broad generalizations	• Applies generalizations appropriately as they apply to the big picture

(cont.)

Table 3.1   Stages of Motivation and Behavioral Characteristics (Cont.)

	Stage 1 *Self-Absorbed*	Stage 2 *Approval Oriented*	Stage 3 *Relationship Oriented*	Stage 4 *Others Oriented*
Identifying Behavioral Characteristics	• Has difficulty generalizing	• Makes limited generalizations	• Able to make fairly broad generalizations	• Applies generalizations appropriately as they apply to the big picture
	• Has difficulty seeing how one problem causes another	• Sees some connection between problems	• Has an understanding of the interrelationships of problems	• Quickly sees the interrelationships of problems
	• May lack basic knowledge	• May have maintained basic knowledge, but lacks confidence	• Possesses knowledge and wants competence respected	• Is willing to share knowledge with others
	• Often bases answers on an incomplete understanding	• Is able to construct limited interpretations	• Will withhold judgment until all information is received	• Is able to make ad hoc interpretations seeking help when necessary
	• Requires close supervision to maintain effort	• Needs supportive supervision	• Works well with intermittent supervision	• Works best without supervision
	• Believes what he or she sees	• Attempts to explain unexpected events but looks for approval in doing so	• Is willing to risk confidently	• Very empathetic
	• Is easily defeated with difficult tasks	• Can become frustrated with difficult tasks but will come around if encouraged by others	• Can delay gratification to continue working on difficult tasks	• Is seldom frustrated with difficult tasks
	• Blames others for failure or difficulty	• Accepts some responsibility for mistakes	• Accepts responsibility for mistakes	• Quickly accepts responsibility for mistakes
	• Has difficulty following directions	• Is concerned about being right	• Is careful about following directions	• Is creative in solving problems
	• Sees teaching as difficult	• Sees teaching as difficult, but doable with support	• Sees teaching as enjoyable	• Enjoys the challenge of teaching's often difficult tasks

Table 3.2   Stages of Motivation and Appropriate Supervisory Style

	Stage 1 Self-Absorbed	Stage 2 Approval Oriented	Stage 3 Relationship Oriented	Stage 4 Others Oriented
Appropriate Supervisory Style	• Supervise closely and provide continual guidance	• Provide moderate supervision	• Emphasize school goals and aspirations	• Supervise minimally
	• Define expectations clearly and precisely, limiting alternatives	• Praise and encourage achievement frequently	• Allow input about rules and expectations	• Make decisions by consensus
	• Establish concise, easily understood rules	• Emphasize personal accomplishment	• Acknowledge teacher as a responsible and competent individual	• Engage in discussions regarding validity of values and standards
	• Clarify and explain goals frequently	• Encourage responsible, independent behavior	• Encourage cooperative problem-solving and group activities	• Present problems and elicit solutions
	• Provide rewards for achievement	• Provide opportunities for recognition	• Provide less direct oversight	• Set goals cooperatively
	• Intervene immediately when problems arise	• Communicate need for improvement, not perfection	• Assure teacher that his or her goals are on target	• Take a supportive role allowing the maximum amount of freedom
	• Teach the skills needed to master new techniques or practices with specific deadlines	• Establish precise expectations	• Communicate personal respect validating ideas and thoughts	• Provide ample opportunities for demonstrating success
	• Maintain strong eye contact when giving instruction	• Allow limited involvement in decision making	• Provide less correction and more information	• Direct teacher toward opportunities to help others in the school or community
	• Break the expectations into smaller steps	• Focus the teacher on living up to school expectations	• Invite participation in setting goals	• When correction is necessary, allow the teacher to devise a solution and a means of remedying the situation
	• Step in quickly to identify the appropriate and inappropriate actions with their accompanying consequences	• Step in quickly to help structure problems areas	• Help the teacher to accept your assistance	• Encourage teacher to assist others

Chapter 4

Four Behavior Styles

Over the years, researchers have identified and divided more than 1,600 personality patterns into four basic behavior styles: self-assertive, socially interactive, analytic, and accommodating. While all four styles are generally blended within any one individual, usually one or two exert the most influence on how that person behaves (Gregorc, 1979; Marston, 1979).

A behavior style is simply a set of observable behaviors, a way to categorize how a person will typically (re)act. Knowing these characteristics can be useful in predicting how that person will tend to communicate, learn, and respond in certain social situations. However, even if you can narrow a teacher's behavior down to one or two most influential styles, principals need to guard against the tendency to put someone in a box. No one is locked into one or two specific styles as they will not always respond in the same way. They often tend to manifest different characteristics depending on the setting. For example, some adults behave quite differently at work and at home just as some students are seemingly different people with their friends and with their parents. Successful relationships depend on how well the principal is able to communicate with teachers manifesting each behavior style.

We have identified two dimensions of behavior that help to clarify the nuances of different personality tendencies: directiveness and responsiveness. Generally, people who want to control their environment are more directive, while those who adapt readily to their environment are more responsive. These dimensions are independent of each other and remain more or less constant throughout one's life. When the four basic behavior styles are placed in quadrants relative to these dimensions (see Figure 4.1), it becomes relatively easy to predict how people will behave in most situations.

In general, the population is equally divided into the four quadrants, and no gender or racial group dominates any one. Each quadrant has both positive and negative characteristics and no one style or dimension is better than another. There are, however, situations where one style is more effective than another. As people become more self-confident, they learn to adapt their behavior style to the situation and to use the style that is most effective.

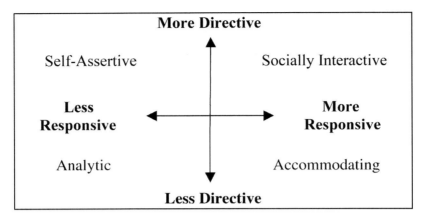

Figure 4.1   Directiveness versus Responsiveness

Characteristics of the four behavior styles are detailed in Table 4.1, which provides further insight into the dimensions of directiveness and responsiveness. We have categorized the behavior style by emotional needs, general characteristics, strengths, weaknesses, communication style, and preferred learning styles. Again, these are tendencies that can change depending upon the setting and circumstances of a particular situation.

Once you have identified a teacher's stage of motivation and the prevalent behavior style, a personality profile will begin to emerge (see Table 4.2). With this information, you will be equipped to identify the most effective methods of communication, to select appropriate motivational strategies, to avoid creating stress and additional behavioral problems, and to utilize the most effective supervisory style.

As you begin assessing the profile of others, it remains critical that you again self-reflect to determine where you fall in this spectrum. Once you do, you will be much more effective as you guide and encourage teachers in their growth.

CHAPTER 4 QUESTIONS TO PONDER

1. In self-reflection, which behavior style most accurately reflects my professional behavior?
2. How do I adapt my behavior style to meet the needs of others as necessary?
3. Do I tend to be more directive or more responsive?
4. What can I do to get out of my comfort zone to most effectively meet the needs of others?
5. As I assess others, do I put them in a box and if so, what can I do to change that?

Table 4.1 Behavior Style Characteristics

	Self-Assertive	Socially Interactive	Analytic	Accommodating
Emotional Needs	• Admiration • Recognition • Authority • Autonomy	• Appreciation • Recognition • Attention • Sociability	• Being understood • Affirmation • Close personal relationships • Order	• Stable relationships • Stable environment • Structure • Caring atmosphere
General Characteristics	• Extroverted • Highly directive • Controls to obtain results	• Extroverted • Moderately responsive • Strives for personal impact on others	• Introverted • Moderately directive • Attempts to control self and immediate environment	• Introverted • Highly responsive • Needs to belong
Strengths	• Gets immediate results • Assumes authority and guides projects through sheer determination • Motivates others through his/her visionary abilities • Completes tasks even amid criticism • Initiates action once his/her vision is shared • Enjoys change and accepts new challenges • Makes quick decisions • Enjoys solving problems • Likes to take risks • Enjoys competition • Is innovative • Prefers short projects	• Is warm and outgoing • Verbalizes well and is articulate • Is the life of the party-witty and exuberant • Approaches tasks intuitively and emotionally • Has an energetic enthusiasm that can excite others • Is optimistic • Makes a favorable impression • Is compassionate • Enjoys contact with others • Sells ideas • Is a team planner • Enjoys giving demonstrations	• Excels at analytic projects • Enjoys working under familiar circumstances • Is cautious • Excels in low-risk environment • Is diplomatic • Is devoted • Is creative • Pays attention to details, directives, and standards • Is persistent and not easily exasperated • Checks for accuracy and consistency • Is orderly and organized • Maintains a very pleasing work environment • Adheres to rules	• Works according to a pattern • Is able to remain in one place or position • Doesn't get too excited • Is patient and rarely angers • Tends to be very stable • Has a dry sense of humor • Avoids getting involved in activities • Listens and concentrates well • Is responsive • Is calm and able to calm others • Is diplomatic, practical, and objective • Encourages loyalty among those he/she controls • Accepts change very slowly; is very cautious

(cont.)

Table 4.1 Behavior Style Characteristics (Cont.)

	Self-Assertive	Socially Interactive	Analytic	Accommodating
Weaknesses	• Ignores the needs of others when moving ahead on projects • Is too forceful, even domineering • May be prone to angry outbursts, but usually has self-control • Deals harshly with others when they don't reach the goals he/she has set for them • Retains grudges • Wants his/her own way immediately • Confronts others by beginning with a personal attack	• Fluctuates emotionally • May be impulsive and make snap decisions • May be egocentric • May not follow through with projects • Oversells himself/herself • Lacks attention to detail • Prone to waste time talking	• Fluctuates emotionally—highs and lows can be significant • Is perfectionistic • Is indecisive • Is overly sensitive to criticism • Lacks sense of humor • May be perceived as unsociable • May ask too many questions • Tends to over check information	• Is insecure • Conforms too easily; can be manipulated • Lacks self-confidence • Rates the opinions of others too highly • Worries; can be unsettled • Procrastinates and misses opportunities • Lacks sense of urgency
Communication Style	• Communicates forcefully; gets right to the point • Converses efficiently, but tends to interrupt • Discusses results and is action oriented • Uses physical presence to exert control of situation • Maintains direct eye contact • Is impatient with delays	• Excitable • Persuasive • Talkative • Discusses grand dreams and intuitions • Physically expressive • Uses eye contact to enhance rapport	• Speaks slowly and methodically • Speaks seriously • Is detail oriented and thorough • Discusses concepts, thoughts, and ideas • Shows little emotion • Avoids eye contact	• Uses an easy, relaxed tone of voice • Is patient • Discusses feelings and relationships • Avoids confrontational conversations • Has a relaxed posture • Avoids eye contact if the relationship is strained
Preferred Learning Style	• Seeks utility • Needs to know how things work • Processes information abstractly and actively • Focuses on one thing at a time • Enjoys problem-solving • Prefers to work with unambiguous ideas • Likes discovery-oriented inquiry • Enjoys working on independent projects • Likes to initiate discussion	• Seeks creative options • Needs to know the purpose of things • Processes information concretely and actively • Enjoys variety • Thrives on spontaneity; is adaptable • Enjoys learning, particularly in groups and in open-ended projects • Likes teaching others	• Listens to and forms theories, concepts, and principles • Seeks facts and continuity of ideas • Values expert opinions • Needs detail • Thinks sequentially and analytically • Processes information abstractly and reflectively • Is interested in ideas rather than people • Enjoys the traditional classroom setting	• Seeks clarity and meaning • Becomes personally and emotionally involved • Listens and shares ideas • Is interested in people and cultures • Processes information concretely and reflectively • Enjoys group projects but individual responsibility • Prefers orderly presentations • Likes "hands-on" learning

Table 4.2 Profiles by Motivation Stage and Behavior Style

	Behavior Style			
	Self-Assertive	**Socially Interactive**	**Analytic**	**Accommodating**
Stage 1 - Self-Absorbed	• Does not generally seek help • Attempts tasks or projects without understanding them • Needs ongoing evaluation • Tends not to pay attention to details, but simply finishes the task • Responds quickly—either positively or negatively—in a very assertive way • Maintains his/her position even when there is strong evidence against it • Becomes very oppositional if challenged • Expends purposeful effort only when convinced of benefit • Attempts to direct or lead • Desires proof to back up questionable statements from others	• Avoids detail work • Tends to be unaware of time • Tries to socialize too much • Asks "what if?" questions • May let desire for popularity get in the way of doing a task • Is enthusiastic • Is talkative • Is overly confident • Is outgoing • Needs goals and objectives	• Needs low-risk situations • Needs a lot of explanation • Needs organization • Likes rules and standards • Needs encouragement • Likes step-by-step procedures • Likes low-stress work • Tends to ask too many questions • May check and recheck finished work • Needs to feel safe	• Needs time to adjust to a new task • Is cautiously willing • Is likely to procrastinate • Needs understanding • Is productive if expectations are moderate • Lacks a sense of urgency • Does not require purpose in order to engage in a project or activity • Prefers working alone to working with others
Stage 2 - Approval Oriented	• Focuses on the task at the expense of other people or other responsibilities • Wants to direct others even when not in a leadership role • Tends to be overzealous when competing	• Gets along well with others • Helps others look on the positive side • Tries to gain popularity • Is a good spokesperson • Is persuasive • Likes to talk	• Avoids unpleasantness with others • Likes regimentation • Spends a lot of time on details • May overdo planning before making a decision • Tends to be serious	• Is amiable • Prefers to work alone when new tasks are being learned • Is low key when working with others • Likes to be part of a social group

(cont.)

Table 4.2 Profiles by Motivation Stage and Behavior Style (Cont.)

	Behavior Style			
	Self-Assertive	**Socially Interactive**	**Analytic**	**Accommodating**
Stage 2 - Approval Oriented	• Likes to know exactly what is to be accomplished • Takes risks—even if inappropriate • Wants to be perceived as powerful • Tends to be very determined • Is very observant • May be reluctant to begin a new task for fear that it might draw negative attention	• Likes to be neighborly • Engages in attention-getting behavior • Likes to be with people at the expense of finishing a task • Is trusting	• Is very respectful • May have difficulty in groups in which tasks are delegated • May be too cautious about joining in with others	• Becomes stubborn if pushed • May not communicate vital information to others • May not like to share credit • Avoids leadership role • Does not like change • Likes to be appreciated
Stage 3 - Relationship Oriented	• Likes to delegate • Is very straightforward • Accepts challenges readily • Likes short, clear presentations • Likes and needs to be involved in decision making • May be overly directive when working with groups • May be abrupt when ready to move on to another task • Likes authority • Prefers short-term projects	• Likes to look successful • Likes recognition • Likes acceptance • May be overly optimistic • Needs goals and objectives • May be persuasive without sound reasoning • May want more group discussion than is needed • May talk too much • Loves exciting projects	• Likes research projects • Is cooperative • Needs reasons for activity • Tends to have a narrow focus • Needs thinking time • Needs standard operating procedures • May get tense at times if under stress • May be overly cautious when making joint decisions • Tries to reduce risk in decisions	• Is sincere • Is willing • Is dedicated • Is loyal • Is a good listener • Enjoys stable, routine tasks in cooperative groups • May procrastinate if expectations are too high • Is prone to listen while others make decisions • Is very patient with others • Is empathetic

Stage 4 - Others Oriented

- Likes independence
- Likes to set his/her own pace
- May overlook details
- Prefers activity over lengthy discussions
- Is very productive
- Presents his/her point of view with strong conviction
- Accepts responsibility and leadership gladly
- Tends to be an opinion leader
- Organizes others effectively

- Benefits from assistance in managing time
- Desires other's support in setting goals and objectives
- Likes to spend time with others
- Is very careful about making unpleasant decisions
- Prefers working with others
- Motivates people
- Needs to plan and concentrate on projects
- Invests himself/herself in meaningful tasks
- Needs to be more realistic about time needed to complete tasks or projects

- Is sensitive to others' feelings when offering suggestions
- Avoids risky decisions
- Checks with others for confirmation regarding difficult decisions
- Desires more information than most others
- Strives for perfection in form, procedure, and detail
- Is very idealistic
- Is extremely loyal
- Plans and executes projects well
- Is highly dependable

- Tentative about making decisions that involve change
- May put off unpleasant decisions too long
- Is very diplomatic
- Is exceptionally patient
- Tends to be very well organized
- Needs additional time to respond to pressure situations
- Is very dependable
- Is most effective when handling one project at a time
- Tends to be comfortable with the status quo

Chapter 5

Quality Teaching Indicators

Before focusing on specific individual challenges and their subsequent intervention strategies, we begin by looking at the goal of quality teaching indicators. Quality teachers manifest many skills and attributes that make them outstanding. While it is possible to enumerate a multitude of talents and skills that reflect quality teaching, such a list quickly becomes unwieldy and loses focus in developing the wholeness needed to contribute to the overall development of teacher success. We have found that quality teaching indicators cluster into four major skills: Workmanship, Self-Control, Relationship, and Caring (see Textbox 5.1).

Workmanship Skills: Embody the characteristics essential to being a skillful, artful, and committed teacher.

Self-Control Skills: Demonstrate the emotional maturity of an individual, often seen in a teacher's ability to self-assess and be self-disciplined.

Relationship Skills: Exhibit effective communication abilities that allow one to encourage and motivate others such as listening intently, giving appropriate feedback, and engaging in productive problem-solving.

Caring Skills: Exemplify a deep appreciation of another's situation characteristically resulting in action taken that truly helps another feel loved and appreciated.

The primary pillars of teacher success, these four skill clusters are clear indicators of whether an individual is truly an exceptional teacher or if and in what areas he or she may need additional assistance. By focusing on these four areas, it is possible to develop training and intervention strategies that contribute to both school and individual success, but first, one must ascertain how you align these Skill Clusters with the Behavior Styles.

ALIGNING THE SKILL CLUSTERS WITH THE BEHAVIOR STYLES

Our research has led us to believe that certain behavior styles naturally align with certain skill clusters. For example, a teacher with a Self-Assertive behavior style will tend to have a closer affinity for Workmanship rather than Caring skills. The reason for this is primarily in the behavioral characteristics for the Self-Assertive style which tend toward an active/competitive involvement in tasks. While this affinity can take on a negative aspect if the teacher is operating at a lower stage of motivation, it is the area in which one would most likely see initial growth when the teacher becomes more mature and demonstrates more positive characteristics.

Like the affinity of the Self-Assertive teacher for Workmanship skills, other behavior styles also have preferences. People with a Socially Interactive style tend to have an affinity for Relationship traits. The reason for this is again found in their behavior style. In their desire to make friends with others, socially interactive people are, as a rule extroverted, warm, outgoing, and highly sociable.

Analytic people have an affinity for Self-Control traits. Desiring order, these individuals often attempt to control themselves and their environment in an effort to maintain continuity and adhere to the rules. They try very hard to avoid conflict and tend to be very diplomatic in their responses to others, and more often than not, this is done displaying the minimum of emotion.

Having a high affinity for Caring traits, people with the Accommodating style are highly interested in feelings and are careful to avoid hurting others. Highly responsive and very patient, they are good listeners and have the ability to feel someone else's pain.

Since all people have secondary behavior styles, it is often true that they will have some affinity for clusters other than the one directly related to their primary style.

While the Individualized Intervention Strategy System focuses on specific problem issues, supervisors who see the specific presenting problem as part of a larger issue, such as Self-Control or Caring, are able to develop additional strategies or interventions that deal with not only the presenting problem but with the larger issue as well. This then maximizes leadership effectiveness.

Expanding the descriptions of the skills underlying each of the four pillars as they relate to teachers helps principals better meet the needs of those they lead.

WORKMANSHIP SKILLS

Qualities that demonstrate competence and the motivation to insure that things are done in an effective and efficient manner, workmanship skills are essential to one's success in any profession. A teacher with good workmanship skills

1. Understands and keeps abreast of the academic discipline and is able to use this understanding to create new learning experiences;
2. Understands how students develop and provides learning opportunities supporting that growth;
3. Utilizes a variety of instructional strategies to benefit student learning;

4. Creates a positive and motivating classroom environment;
5. Seeks to contribute to the effectiveness of the school in an active manner;
6. Possesses planning and organizational skills;
7. Is an active problem solver; and
8. Is flexible and adaptable in managing priorities.

As a principal probes to determine the level of competence a teacher possesses, he or she is also trying to gauge the underlying attributes that will empower the teacher to become one of quality and one who can become a teacher leader in the school. Here are some workmanship qualities to look for and questions to ask as you begin to assess your faculty:

1. Foresight: Do they seek opportunities to help others and participate in a helpful manner?
2. Self-starter: Do they take initiative for starting and finishing tasks?
3. Organized: Do they plan and organize themselves and their classes in a systematic manner?
4. Dependable: Can they be counted on to uphold commitments and expectations?
5. Responsible: Will they accept responsibility for their students, materials, behaviors, and assignments related to their roles?
6. Perseverant: Will they follow through regardless of the task or relationship difficulties?

SELF-CONTROL SKILLS

Self-control skills are often somewhat difficult to ascertain because many times it is only in stressful situations that one can see the level of self-control a person actually possesses. A teacher with good self-control skills

1. Manages his or her impulsivity and distressed emotions even in tense situations;
2. Can be counted on to act in a truthful and ethical manner;
3. Has an open mind and is not quick to judge;
4. Is quick to take responsibility for personal actions;
5. Demonstrates strong convictions and loyalty to the organization and people within;
6. Accepts opposition without personalizing it; and
7. Adapts and is flexible to benefit others.

Here are some self-control attributes to look for and questions to ask as you begin to assess your faculty:

1. Restrained: Do they accept disagreement and conflict in a controlled manner, not personalizing it?
2. Open: Do they maintain an open mind, not judging the beliefs and actions of others without good cause?
3. Principled: Do they live by a set of principles, beliefs, and values?

4. Committed: Do they have strong convictions and remain steadfast to those even in the face of adversity?
5. Rule abiding: Do they have a strong sense of right and wrong, never breaking rules without good reason?
6. Compliant: Do they willingly accept rules and regulations?
7. Easygoing: Do they remain even tempered, not being easily offended or excited in the face of opposition?
8. Accountable: Do they accept responsibility for actions even if it means the disapproval of others?
9. Truthful: Are they honest to the point of even avoiding exaggeration?
10. Flexible: Are they willing to adapt and change if it benefits others?

RELATIONSHIP SKILLS

Relationship skills are probably the primary key to one's success. If a person has good people skills and only moderate workmanship skills, he or she is far more likely to keep his or her job than if the reverse was true under trying circumstances. In fact, if someone cannot get along with others, chances are he or she will often create a toxic working environment, becoming the bane of the principal and staff, rather than a quality teacher. A teacher with good relationship skills

1. Communicates thoughts and feelings effectively;
2. Wins people over;
3. Handles difficult people in a positive manner;
4. Listens actively;
5. Engages in open debate on issues without turning them into a win/lose situation;
6. Makes friends and builds social networks;
7. Enjoys working with people and building relationships with them;
8. Motivates others and helps create opportunities for change and growth; and
9. Makes the work environment a pleasant and inviting place.

Here are some relationship attributes to look for and questions to ask as you begin to assess your faculty:

1. Forthright: Do they state the truth while not taking advantage of a situation for personal gain?
2. Sensitive: Do they respect others while treating them with dignity?
3. Considerate: Do they focus on the needs of others?
4. Inclusive: Can they relate to all groups and actively include them in activities?
5. Loyal: Do they stand up for others, not abandoning them even when it may have a negative personal impact?
6. Discreet: Do they avoid talking about others behind their backs or sharing information that may impact them negatively?
7. Honest: Can they be depended on to be honest, not expanding upon the truth for effect or personal gain?

8. Agreeable: Do they make a concerted effort to get along with others even in difficult situations?
9. Humble: Do they give deference to others, not thinking too highly of themselves?

CARING SKILLS

Caring skills are those often intangible skills that make people feel like they belong and are an invitation to others to become a vital part of the school or other type of organization. They are the glue that holds the school together: faculty, staff, and students. In a society that is loaded with many unsettling social issues such as the loss of jobs, family violence, and divorce, the value of caring cannot be underestimated. A teacher with good caring skills

1. Understands others by sensing their needs and showing an active interest and concern for them;
2. Reaches out to others to meet their needs in a positive and uplifting manner;
3. Becomes an advocate for others who may not be able to advocate for themselves;
4. Demonstrates tolerance for others' views and actions that are different or even unsettling;
5. Demonstrates sensitivity toward others' weaknesses preserving their dignity;
6. Demonstrates mercy for others; and
7. Invests in helping others develop to their fullest potential.

Here are some caring attributes to look for and questions to ask as you begin to assess your faculty:

1. Sympathetic: Are they sensitive to the needs of others while caring for them?
2. Forgiving: Do they forgive others' offenses, while not becoming resentful?
3. Respectful: Do they show respect for authority and for others they encounter?
4. Nonjudgmental: Do they demonstrate grace and sensitivity by not judging others quickly or negatively?
5. Optimistic: Do they look on the bright side of things and maintain a positive view even in the face of negative occurrences?
6. Kind: Are they sensitive to others, displaying gentleness in dealing with difficult situations involving them?
7. Sincere: Do they say things they believe to be true?
8. Tolerant: Are they accepting of others' opinions and behaviors?
9. Available: Are they accessible to others showing little concern for their own needs and desires?
10. Trusting: Do they accept others at face value, not prematurely judging them?

Representing the foundational principles or quality teaching indicators that determine teacher success, these four skill clusters serve as a guide to better understand teacher needs and motivations. In this understanding, one is able to identify possible strengths and needs of individuals on the teaching team to determine the best strategies to facilitate positive teacher growth.

PROMOTING GROWTH IN THE SKILL CLUSTERS

The goal of any principal is to promote growth within his or her building in order to create a quality school, and while the heart of the leader is critical in setting the environmental tone, that is only the beginning. It is important for the principal to become very familiar with the principles associated with each of the four skill clusters. By connecting these principles to each of the four pillars of teacher quality, we believe we can maximize their effectiveness and can focus the use of the principles in a manner that relates them to specific outcomes. These principles are intended to create an ethos in the school and to build a climate of success and partnership that transcends the issues and challenges related to the day-to-day operation of a school.

ENCOURAGING WORKMANSHIP SKILLS BY MOTIVATION STAGE AND BEHAVIOR STYLE

One would think that all teachers would possess good workmanship skills, but in actuality, there are many who could become better teachers if they were to seek improvement in this area. This may be true for some principals as well.

Workmanship skills are generally evident in a purposeful, clearly planned, and well-ordered environment. This requires a sense of vision, attention to detail, and an ongoing management system. Principals who desire to encourage workmanship must first be sure they are practicing those same traits themselves. Much like children, teachers and staff will model what they *see*, not what they are *told*. As a principal, you encourage and facilitate good workmanship skills when you

1. Establish clear goals and objectives for the school each year and revisit those regularly to monitor growth.
2. Facilitate teacher planning and organization through regular classroom visitations to offer encouragement and gauge progress.
3. Communicate clear standards and expectations as to how the school will operate and ensure that those standards are managed in an equitable manner.
4. Provide prompt feedback to teachers regarding issues and questions.
5. Make sure teachers know their efforts in the classroom and school are useful and meaningful and not just busy work.
6. Help teachers accurately self-assess in an open and nonjudgmental way so they willingly do so without fear of retribution or condemnation.
7. Empower teachers to assume responsibility and decision making in the life of the school.
8. Encourage risk taking by not only encouraging it, but also by making it safe to embark upon it.
9. Respond with "what happened" rather than "what did you do" when mistakes happen, which builds esprit de corps and motivate people to commit themselves to the organization even more.
10. Celebrate with teachers and staff when they have success, remembering you are merely the facilitator of their success, not the owner.

11. Maintain a positive and encouraging manner even in the darkest of times.
12. Treat every teacher as a valued contributor not only to the school but to you personally.
13. Assume the responsibility when things don't turn out as they should, not throwing teachers and staff under the bus.
14. Instill a spirit of cooperation by encouraging and promoting working together.
15. Reinforce the concept of team, downplaying the "I" while encouraging faculty and staff to join together in accomplishing the objectives that have been mutually agreed upon.
16. Remember to use the term "we" rather than "my," communicating a team effort of shared responsibility rather than a sense of personal ownership, which mitigates against a sense of community and belongingness.

After a school leader implements this posture in his or her everyday skills and practice, in terms of workmanship skills, it is helpful to recognize the various actions associated with each of the stages of motivation and their accompanying behavior style (see Table 5.1).

ENCOURAGING SELF-CONTROL SKILLS BY MOTIVATION STAGE AND BEHAVIOR STYLE

Self-control is a quality admired by everyone yet too often lost in fast-moving, stressful situations. A good maxim to remember is that emotions never grow up; they are simply manifested in a different way. In today's litigious world, self-control is a particularly prized virtue. As a principal, you encourage and facilitate good self-control skills when you

1. Show appreciation for respectful behavior at all times, but particularly those that are stressful.
2. Help teachers understand and implement effective conflict management techniques, not assuming they know them.
3. Engage in problem-solving exercises with teachers and staff around issues that directly affect them so they feel free to share and seek out counselors when difficult scenarios arise.
4. Help teachers develop a long-range perspective rather than always expecting a quick resolution.
5. Maintain a calm authority in crisis situations, while ensuring the safety and security of all.
6. Learn everything possible about complainers and their grievances in order to understand the issues and the basic attitudes behind the criticism with the goal of developing a common ground for moving forward.
7. Avoid power struggles when decisions are under fire. Explain decisions and, when appropriate, the rationale behind them, but don't justify or apologize. This shows deference and respect while signaling an openness and willingness to hear concerns.

8. Encourage responsibility for one's actions and focus on the behavior and not the excuse, leaving people with their self-respect rather than denigration.

9. Criticize the task and not the person. Be as positive as possible with your admonitions and advice.

10. Respond in a measured way rather than react to criticism by taking time to gain composure and accepting responsibility for your own actions. If in error, apologize for your actions.

11. Make sure all the facts are gathered before correction is given. Be consistent, dispassionate, and immediate whenever possible, always ending on a positive and upbeat note and respecting the individual.

12. Create a sense of success when teachers and staff demonstrate self-control, which not only encourages the proper handling of difficult situations but also sets the standard.

After a school leader implements this posture in their everyday skills and practice, in terms of self-control skills, it is helpful to recognize the various actions associated with each of the stages of motivation and their accompanying behavior style (see Table 5.2).

ENCOURAGING RELATIONSHIP SKILLS BY MOTIVATION STAGE AND BEHAVIOR STYLE

There is an old adage: when you die, they won't read your resume at the funeral, they will talk about your relationships. As a principal, this adage should be foremost in your mind if you desire to build a close-knit school. A school that functions based on relationships is one that is most enduring and meaningful for all concerned. As a principal, you encourage and facilitate good relationship skills when you

1. Communicate effectively by remembering how *you* communicate is more important than how someone responds. Be sure you do so in a loving, positive manner, ensuring your message is heard and received accurately. This will clarify ambiguities and will solve many problems associated with miscommunication.

2. Prefer people to performance. Make sure teachers and staff know that they are more important than the tasks.

3. Don't jump to conclusions. Make sure you gather all the facts and the conditions surrounding an incident.

4. Own your mistakes by accepting responsibility for them.

5. Learn to question appropriately. Don't ask questions that are loaded, filled with stress, or lead you to get your preferred answer. Ask those that validate, encourage, and plead for a thoughtful response.

6. Create an atmosphere of respect and caring while engaging teachers and staff in a manner that fosters bonding, camaraderie, and harmony.

7. Provide opportunities for faculty and staff to get together to work on projects, to socialize, and to work on team building. This affirms each of the staff members while creating a collective bond.

8. Build trusting relationships by being open, honest, and encouraging.

9. Share with the faculty and staff as much about decisions or the future plans as is possible. The more you are willing and able to share information and to seek input, the more open, honest, and trusting the staff will become.
10. Don't let misunderstandings fester. Deal with them immediately in a positive, forthright, and honest manner.
11. Find ways to celebrate teacher accomplishments by encouraging them to present at workshops and conferences or to speak or demonstrate their skills at community events. This projects a sense of pride and confidence in them.
12. Encourage shared governance of the school by involving teachers in as many planning and decision-making activities as is reasonable and appropriate.
13. Involve faculty in the hiring of new teachers. This builds a sense of esprit de corps and creates an attitude of excellence. Teachers want the best for their school and this affirms them as they select the best for their school.
14. Encourage mentoring relationships among the teachers and staff. Create the attitude that we are all in this together and whatever we can do to help one another, we will do.
15. Don't allow teachers to become isolated. Instead, involve them immediately in the fabric of the school. Especially with new teachers, come alongside them and ensure that they are handling the learning curve and be sure to provide them help quickly if you sense they are struggling.
16. Allow your love for the staff and students to show by your caring, your buoyant attitude, and your ability to laugh and keep things in perspective.

After a school leader implements this posture in their everyday skills and practice, in terms of relationship skills, it is helpful to recognize the various actions associated with each of the stages of motivation and their accompanying behavior style (see Table 5.3).

ENCOURAGING CARING SKILLS BY MOTIVATION STAGE AND BEHAVIOR STYLE

The statement "People don't care about how much you know until they know how much you care" is no more valid than in a school. A principal who lives this creates a milieu within the school that is loving, trusting, open, and effective. As a principal, you encourage and facilitate good caring skills when you

1. Acknowledge considerate attitudes when you see them demonstrated, setting in place an attitude that permeates the entire school and quickly becomes the norm.
2. Demonstrate a heartfelt interest and concern for teachers and staff validating and exemplifying a genuine commitment to them beyond just the professional level.
3. Practice an open-door policy by making yourself available to listen, advise, and counsel when necessary.
4. Provide little acts of kindness and grace when dealing with personal matters that require flexibility and special consideration. You will reap a great harvest in both good will and commitment if you go that extra mile.

5. Forgive when things don't go as planned and feelings get hurt. It is a powerful tool and one that says "I love you" regardless.

6. Treat poor performance as an opportunity to learn and grow and not a "gotcha" moment. In these cases, provide whatever assistance is necessary to give a teacher the opportunity to be successful.

7. Approach a termination situation in a manner that is respectful, making leaving as painless as possible. Provide assistance in moving on and don't react to the push back that might occur during times like this. You must clearly be the adult. Try to make it a beneficial experience even if in the short term; it may not seem that way. Always leave the person with dignity and self-respect.

8. Practice active listening. Let people say what they desire without interruptions and without providing them with a solution when all they want is to be heard.

9. Share your goals, thoughts, feelings, and expectations with the staff and invite them to do the same with you and with each other. Too often we don't openly address the things that are closest to our hearts but instead focus primarily on the tasks before us. By laying out a picture of what we would like to be, a new and committed spirit envelops the school and people come together to create a shared vision.

10. Actively encourage tolerance and understanding of differences among faculty, staff, and students.

11. Demonstrate respect for others' feelings, and name the emotions you and the staff members may be experiencing providing validation for the person, their feelings, and the reason behind their feelings.

12. Use notes to express sympathy, congratulations, or encouragement. Words are helpful, but a written note demonstrates a depth of caring far beyond.

13. Practice empathy, not sympathy, when comforting staff in a tense situation. Sympathy puts you in the same place and feeling the same issues as the individual you are comforting, often blurring your rational thoughts concerning the issue. Empathy, on the other hand, allows you to reach out to comfort another without getting so caught up in the emotional feelings to the point that you lose your objectivity and ability to maintain your problem-solving abilities.

14. Always listen for the emotions behind a person's words. This allows you to deal with the feeling as well as the issue. By identifying the emotions, you can deescalate issues that could not be handled by a rational response. You need to respond to many issues both on an emotional level and in an objective manner.

After a school leader implements this posture in their everyday skills and practice, in terms of caring skills, it is helpful to recognize the various actions associated with each of the stages of motivation and their accompanying behavior style (see Table 5.4).

Once you are familiar with the quality teaching indicators and their four skill clusters, it's time to focus on some more specific problematic teacher issues.

CHAPTER 5 QUESTIONS TO PONDER

1. Which quality teaching indicators do I value most? Why?
2. Do I feel more comfortable with the characteristics and attributes associated with one skill cluster over another? Does this align with my own behavior style?
3. What can I do to ensure that I most appropriately meet the needs of all the teachers and staff in the building for which I am responsible?
4. What specifically do I do to encourage workmanship? Self-Control? Relationship? Caring?
5. How can I personally grow in these areas so I can best meet the needs of the teachers in my care?

Table 5.1　Workmanship Skills by Motivation Stage and Behavior Style

	Behavior Style			
	Self-Assertive	Socially Interactive	Analytic	Accommodating
Self-Absorbed	• Pushes ahead without proper understanding • Can be overly confident • Doesn't pay attention to details • Likes to work independently • Likes to complete tasks quickly	• Tends to be disorganized • Avoids detail work • Needs structure to get started • Asks a lot of questions	• Quits easily if not supported • Is overly perfectionistic • Personalizes criticism • Can be negative about assignments	• Is fearful about taking on challenging tasks • Procrastinates • May make excuses if things don't go well
Approval Oriented	• Determined to accomplish a task, but needs to know exactly what it is • Will procrastinate if the challenge is too great • Can get negative if he or she fails to accomplish task successfully • Is learning to problem solve with others • Will shift blame if not successful	• Tends to be adaptable and works well with others • Likes to participate in discussions • Has improving organizational skills • Will make excuses for failure • Likes exciting projects	• Is compliant • Is purposeful when attempting tasks • Demonstrates good insight • Follows through • Is diligent • May ask many questions	• Can be productive if expectations are moderate • Is very respectful of authority • Needs supportive approach to persevere • Is very adaptable • Tends to have good insights • Tends to be punctual • Works best in orderly situations • Will engage in tasks if assured that praise and reward are forthcoming • Likes to handle one task at a time
Relationship Oriented	• Can be depended on to complete task • May become overly directive if things don't happen as expected • Prefers short-term tasks • Has improving organizational skills • Is decisive, but adaptable as well	• Likes to work with others • Is very cooperative • Can work independently • Is conscious of details and realizes the need to recheck work • Has creative way of looking at assignments • Is able to deal with critiques	• Is very efficient • Seems secure in group settings • Is dependable • Demonstrates a sense of integrity • Evaluates tasks and issues realistically	• Works well in groups • Feels personally responsible for completion of tasks • Works efficiently • Demonstrates a high sense of resourcefulness • Is well organized
Others Oriented	• Very thorough • Has high sense of ethics • Will be truthful in assessment of quality • Accepts responsibility • Is committed to completing a task regardless of challenge • Will accept constructive criticism	• Patient with unclear assignments • Willingly seeks help • Completes assignments on time • Perseveres with difficult tasks • Keeps atmosphere light but productive	• Takes initiative • Maintains calm exterior even with difficult tasks • Is humble about accomplishments • Is very resourceful • Perseveres regardless of difficulty	• Is very diligent • Possesses good planning skills • Is very supportive and encouraging of others • Is very dependable

Table 5.2 Self-Control Skills by Motivation Stage and Behavior Style

	Behavior Style			
	Self-Assertive	**Socially Interactive**	**Analytic**	**Accommodating**
Self-Absorbed	• Resists demands contrary to preferences • Becomes angry if crossed • Has difficulty accepting correction • Sees flexibility as a weakness • Weighs everything against self-interest • Has difficulty accepting others' opinions • Becomes competitive when challenged	• Tends to talk too much • Can be overly enthusiastic • Would rather play than work • Gets bored easily • Has trouble accepting responsibility for actions • Is easily distracted	• Is overly sensitive to criticism and will withdraw quickly • Has a tendency to ask too many detailed questions • Can be very judgmental of others' behavior • Gets frustrated easily if there is a lack of understanding	• Withdraws from pressure situations • Internalizes anger • Conforms too easily to avoid confrontation
Approval Oriented	• Is becoming somewhat adaptable, thereby increasing self-control • Has difficulty handling and being flexible with people who have other behavior styles • Will be respectful if sense mutual respect	• Can be kept on task through close supervision • Tends to charm his or her way out of trouble • Attempts to minimize offenses and weaknesses by downplaying them • Will stick to things if considered significant	• Perceives small errors as complete failures and rejection • Tends toward perfectionism and can become quite exasperated • Appreciates feelings of others	• Prefers to be a group member rather than a leader • Can become sullen if corrected • Will avoid being assertive • Is able to accept criticism if not personal
Relationship Oriented	• Handles frustration well • Is able to accept differences of opinion • Help others sort out choices • Will show leadership with others if competence is clear • Will work with people to achieve a goal even when they are not particularly willing	• Will take responsibility for mistakes and learn from them • Will encourage others to complete tasks and accept responsibility for leadership	• Cooperates well with others • Is very self-disciplined • Is patient • Is adaptable to change	• Is sensitive to others • Will not risk breaking a relationship • Is a peacemaker • Draws others out and is considerate of them • Is extremely tactful
Others Oriented	• Is comfortable with conflict • Thinks logically when under stress • Can handle conflict easily • Can be sensitive to others' feelings • Will not engage in meaningless arguments	• Has developed balance between play and work • Is truthful about issues and takes responsibility for actions • Is humble in accepting praise • Demonstrates the ability to be discreet	• Is able to handle failure and not become overly introspective • Sees criticism as an opportunity to improve • Is very protective of friends • Is fair and equitable with others	• Is loyal to others • Is very sincere • Is very humble • Maintains calm exterior

Table 5.3 Relationship Skills by Motivation Stage and Behavior Style

	Behavior Style			
	Self-Assertive	**Socially Interactive**	**Analytic**	**Accommodating**
Self-Absorbed	• Can be very abrupt with others • Has little patience with others • Can be domineering • May be overly confident of the rightness of his or her feelings • Is insensitive to the needs of others	• Will over-socialize • Needs structure • May tend to be a complainer • May sacrifice truth for popularity • Can be manipulative in relationships	• Desperately needs approval • Tends to be overly sensitive • May evaluate people's behavior a little harshly • Tends to be submissive	• Has difficulty with any unpleasantness • Withdraws quickly if the situation is uncomfortable • Will generally avoid leadership roles in relationships • Tends to blame others for failures in relationships
Approval Oriented	• Communicates feelings in a straightforward manner • Tends to be argumentative • May become belligerent if criticized • Is interested in relationships, but struggles with the equity of meaningful relationships • Is willing to learn from positive role models	• Enjoys being around others • Gets along well with others • May tend to exaggerate things for recognition • Can be very persuasive • May let the desire for popularity get in the way of relationships	• Needs encouragement to make new friends • Is most comfortable with intimate relationships • Will work with others if he or she feels secure • Is patient with others if there is a sense they are trying • Tends to be a little too introspective about relationships	• Needs a very supportive environment • Avoids confrontation • Likes to engage people in nonthreatening conversation • Likes close relationships, particularly with those in authority
Relationship Oriented	• Will respond positively to criticism • Usually takes the leadership role in most social interactions • Makes judgments based on facts, not emotions • Can motivate others • Is able to accept differences of opinion	• Likes to assume lead roles in activities • Demonstrates concern for others • Enjoys cooperative activities • Can be a motivational influence on others • Provides a positive outlook on most things	• Is very self-controlled • Enjoys being in a group setting if the environment is supportive • Reaches out to help others • Is very tactful • Cooperates well with others	• Is a good listener • Is very sensitive to others' emotional needs • Is very available to others • Is extremely considerate • Is quite amiable • Is great mediating when peers disagree • Tends to be able to make peace in difficult situations
Others Oriented	• Is committed to lasting relationships • Handles differences of opinion well • Is motivated to help others • Is a highly effective communicator • Tends to be an opinion leader	• Willingly invests self in helping others • Is able to organize others, but may need some structure • Tends to be very considerate of others, particularly those who struggle • Is a great mediator • Is always available to others	• Is very sensitive to others • Is very sincere and kind • Enjoys deep relationships • Is unusually discreet • Is very loyal and supportive	• Looks out for well-being of others • Will forgive others easily • Is a calm and stable role model for others • Views mistakes as a vehicle for emotional growth and deeper relationships • Acts as a counselor to others

Table 5.4   Caring Skills by Motivation Stage and Behavior Style

	Behavior Style			
	Self-Assertive	**Socially Interactive**	**Analytic**	**Accommodating**
Self-Absorbed	• Has difficulty understanding the feelings of others • Is not tolerant of diverse feelings or thoughts • Will belittle others' opinions • Ignores others' views • Retains grudges	• Can be hypersensitive to perceived rejection and react in kind • Will sacrifice friendships for personal gain • Can be manipulative with people's feelings	• Tends to be reserved in reaching out to others • Can be fearful of exposing concerns • Is hypersensitive to rejection and will end relationships quickly • Can be too overly critical of others if they violate expectations	• Needs personal attention to maintain caring atmosphere • Can become passive-aggressive toward others if he or she senses a lack of appreciation • Will seldom confront others over meaningful issues and can become resentful
Approval Oriented	• Will coerce others into arguments • Will be sensitive to others' views if he or she respects them • Has almost no mercy for others • Has limited ability to appreciate the need to be empathetic	• Is tolerant of others • Demonstrates concern, but tends to be superficial • Sometimes has difficulty understanding own feelings • Will express concern, but will tend not to follow through	• Is compliant with authority • Is generally respectful • Has deeply felt concern for others	• Tends to be available to others • Is very interested in people's needs • Will maintain peace at all costs
Relationship Oriented	• Will make self available to those who need help • Has a cognitive sense of mercy and compassion but not a deep emotional sense • Will give practical steps to solving an issue rather than express empathy	• Is very kind to others • Attempts to help people feel good about each other • Is very loyal to friends • Is fair in dealings with others	• Is becoming content with others and accepts them as they are • Holds high behavior standards for self and can be overly critical of own behavior toward others • Is beginning to realize everything is not all black and white	• Is very tolerant of others • Is concerned for others • Is very sincere • Is extremely patient in dealing with others • Is dedicated to friends
Others Oriented	• Can be understanding, but does not accept an explanation as an excuse for failure • Is tolerant of diverse issues • Can be quite gentle with others • Makes self available to others	• Is consistent with others • Attempts to include everyone in activities • Will befriend those who seem rejected	• Is developing a real sense of forgiveness • Is exceedingly loyal • Is discreet in dealing with others • Looks for ways to help others	• Will do practical things to assist people • Demonstrates a high level of compassion for others • Demonstrates a high degree of mercy regardless of the offense • Will forgive most things, particularly if the other person seems sorry • Is very joyful

Chapter 6

Specific Problematic Teacher Issues

Most people would tend to agree that it is always preferable to focus on positive ways to improve teacher performance, such as strategies to increase motivation and instructional effectiveness, but not always popular to suggest that teachers have challenges and problematic issues that also may need to be addressed. From our collective experience of over a century, we have found that while teachers in general are highly dedicated, skilled professionals, they still experience the demands and problems of adult life. Faculty and staff come to school each day with various personal and/or family issues that can easily spill over into the school setting possibly affecting performance. In addition, professional issues that often accompany life as an educator, such as disagreements with the principal, rifts with colleagues, concerns regarding classroom management, and troubles dealing with difficult parents, may also present challenges. Taken individually or collectively, these trials can create problematic teacher issues, behaviors, or attitudes (see Table 6.1). While these problems are not a reflection of an individual's personal and professional worth, they are however opportunities for improvement and growth of all concerned.

Once a problematic issue is identified and defined, one has a reason to begin the process of the Individualized Intervention Strategy System.

CHAPTER 6 QUESTIONS TO PONDER

1. Am I able to locate the particular problem I am having in this list?
2. If my problem falls outside these parameters, is there a similar one to which it could relate?
3. Am I comfortable beginning this process of the Individualized Intervention Strategy System?

Table 6.1   Problematic Teacher Issues

Problematic Issue	Description
Absenteeism/Tardiness	Frequently absent or chronically late to work
Accountability	Does not hold themselves accountable for the success of their class; Blames the students for failure; Does not feel accountable to the school as a whole
Arrogance	Seems to be above others and the problems faced; Looks down on others
Assessment	Does not assess student progress accurately; Limited methods are used to assess student mastery; Assessments do not align to what was taught
Blame Shifting	Takes no responsibility for own actions; It's always someone else's fault
Classroom Culture	Fails to captivate learners; Sees students who have difficulty only as behavior problems resulting in conflicts; Has an emotionally unsafe classroom (e.g., bullying); Harsh in dealing with students
Classroom Management	Has difficulty with classroom control
Cliquishness	Has a selected group of friends to the exclusion of others
Collegiality	Takes little initiative to relate or collaborate with others ; Not a team player; Not doing his or her share of the load
Compassion	Does not seem to sympathize/empathize with struggling learners, parents, or fellow staff members
Content Knowledge	Demonstrates a lack of understanding of the material; Provides inaccurate, out of date, or wrong information to the students of the subject content
Critical Thinking Skills	Does not evaluate alternative actions; Does not ask important questions of themselves or of their students; Seems to think more linearly
Curriculum	Does not follow prescribed curriculum; May have difficulty establishing and adhering to academic term goals; thus lesson plans are not linked to school/district/state objectives
Disingenuousness	Appears cooperative and supportive in words, but actions are questionable
Disloyalty	Does not cooperate or support those in authority; Publicly and negatively challenges authority or peers
Emotional Inappropriateness	Hypersensitive; Reactive; Defensive; Hot-tempered or volatile; Poor social skills
Exaggeration	Tends to embellish stories or facts about others to the point of "untruth"

Feedback	Does not provide timely feedback; Feedback is often not constructive and sometimes critical
Goal Setting	Does not adequately set goals; Has little or no forward thinking
Gossip	Spreads rumors about others
Impulsivity	Makes decisions without forethought
Indifference	Has no particular interest or concern for others or the institution; Tends to be detrimental to school morale
Inflexibility	Rigid in beliefs and practices; Unwilling to be flexible
Initiative	Does not contribute or take initiative to be a constructive member of the teaching staff
Insensitivity	Unaware or not concerned of others' thoughts and feelings; Unresponsive to other's needs; often lacks tact
Insincerity	Not authentic in communication, both oral and written
Instructional Strategies	Uses a very limited number of instructional strategies; Does not differentiate lessons to meet a variety of student needs
Judgmental	Forms opinions without deliberating facts
Listening	Does not appear to hear or understand the opinions of others
Negativity	Displays a pervasive attitude of negativity toward people, ideas, and tasks; Not encouraging, inspiring, or proactive in teaching
Noncompliance	Does not adhere to the rules, policies, and practices of the school
Parent Interaction	Combative with parents in meetings; Views parents as the enemy rather than as a partner; Does not work to find common ground to solve concerns
Planning Skills	Lesson plans are incomplete or nonexistent; Difficulty with goal formulation; Inability to envision the future for long-term planning
Resentfulness	Is easily offended and appears to hold grudges
Self-centeredness	Does not share vision of the school; Looks out for self at the expense of others; Seldom volunteers for school-sponsored projects
Technology	Does not make use of available technology in lesson planning or other pertinent school activities
Time Management	Does not effectively manage time; Poor pacing of lessons; Late to meetings due to issues in this area
Writing Skills	Does not write well; Includes inappropriate content in their written communications

Chapter 7

The Foundation of the Individualized Intervention Strategy System

Effective supervision is a relationship activity that requires the attention of a caring individual who can both identify and address the need for improvement and structure quality intervention and growth strategies in ways that are sensitive to the needs of both teachers and staff. With that in mind, we intensively studied methods and techniques presented in the research literature on behavioral and motivational change.

SELECTION OF THE STRATEGIES

The range of strategies selected to be included in the "administrative toolbox" emanate from various arenas. For example, clarifying and listening to the person who is having a problem (Sullivan & Glance, 2005) are techniques derived from the counseling field and as previously addressed, active listening skills are essential for the administrator to communicate care and concern for the teacher.

In addition, nonverbal techniques such as the use of gestures, looks, posturing, and proxemics (Sullivan & Glance, 2005) often help deter problems. Even if not completely prevented, the magnitude of the reaction is often decreased if the teacher is cued in a nonthreatening way and without verbal feedback that could be easily misinterpreted. Nonverbal communication is often the first sign to someone that what he or she says or does may be inappropriate.

Other approaches such as the basic review of rules, policies, and expectations (Selig, Arroyo, Lloyd-Zannini, & Jordan, 2006) or the use of humor (McEwan, 2005) are practical in nature and may be viewed as strategies that can stem the tide of difficulties with minimal time expenditure. Such practical approaches are natural to certain principals' temperaments and behavior styles but can be successfully used by all school leaders if correctly delivered.

A variety of teacher supervision techniques have been adapted from the field of educational psychology. For example, Calfee (2006) made an interesting observation when he wrote, "much might be learned from the social cognitive analysis work of teacher leaders, school principals, and superintendents" (p. 36). Strategies such as assigning a mentor, encouraging confidence (i.e., self-efficacy), goal setting, modeling, problem-solving, and providing feedback may be subsumed under the heading of social cognitive approaches.

Additionally, the work of Donald Schon (1996) on reflective practices is represented in several strategies, one of which is reflective journaling, also highlighted in Glickman, Gordon, and Ross-Gordon (2012). Reflections by the teacher concerning the effects of his or her actions, with the addition of feedback and support by the administrator, can be a highly successful strategy for improvement and professional growth (Collet, 2012).

Several of the strategies were taken from collaborative approaches particularly espoused by Glickman et al. (2012), Harris, (2009), and Sullivan and Glance (2005). Collaboration that includes the teacher with the problem, the principal, and other supervisors, and/or other teachers has been used successfully in turning problems into opportunities for growth.

We also borrowed from direct supervision approaches in the areas of problem ownership and committing to a plan of action by the teacher. For example, asking the teacher to accurately define the problem, orally or in written form, and then designing a plan with the supervisor's approval has been successful not only with students but also with school personnel (Cooper, 2003; Ribas, 2005).

INTERVENTION STRATEGIES

Regardless of their origin, effective administrators must not only be prepared to successfully deal with problems as they occur but embrace how these challenges can be turned into opportunities to facilitate teacher growth. Unfortunately, many principals first view a situation as a problem and never see it as an opportunity; oftentimes this occurs because they are not equipped with an array of strategies or tools to deal with an issue. As the old saying goes, "If the only tool you have is a hammer, then every problem looks like a nail." That said, we have provided 43 intervention strategies (see Table 7.1) or tools to add to your "administrative toolbox."

STRATEGY CLASSIFICATION

In order to classify the array of 43 intervention strategies, we adapted Carl Glickman's Supervisory Behavior Continuum (as cited in Glickman et al., 2012), in which they presented 10 categories of supervisory behaviors ranging from listening on one side of the continuum to standardizing and reinforcing on the other side. In our system, we present a four category continuum (Encouraging, Coaching, Structuring, and Directing; see Table 7.2). We have found that limiting the categories to four rather than the more expansive 10 is substantially more efficient to use "on your feet." Also, the four categories further correspond with our Stages of Motivation. For example, teachers who operate from higher stages of motivation are likely to require less intrusive strategies that require a minimum of time and energy expenditure on both the part of the teacher and the principal. These strategies are found in the Encouraging and Coaching categories. On the other hand, teachers who operate from lower stages of motivation will likely require more intrusive strategies listed under Structuring and Directing. In other words, as we move from left to right along the continuum, we are assuming less internal teacher control and thus more supervisor time and influence in a given situation. In reverse, from right to left, the teacher will increase in internal control and regulation and our supervisory role becomes less intrusive and thus less time-consuming.

Our goal was simply to develop a system for determining under what circumstances various approaches would tend to have a higher rate of effectiveness; however, based upon one's particular leadership style, as a principal you may find that some strategies are more or less intrusive than we have suggested. Using this type of system, leaders have combined strategies in unique ways and have even developed some of their own. Because of our experience with the creativeness of leaders and teachers, we encourage you to adapt, modify, and even create new strategies in an effort to find the most effective ways to promote a quality school.

One thing to remember as you begin to implement this system is that one of its catapulting beliefs is that emotions never grow up even though they may play out in quite different ways as people age and mature. Because each person is unique, each strategy must be implemented in light of a person's stage of motivation and behavior style. With that assumption, our goal is to provide tools that will give principals multiple options in handling problematic behaviors as they arise in their schools.

The next chapter is by far the nuts and bolts of the system. With these tools, you as the school leader have all of the pieces to pull the concepts together to meet the needs of the individuals in your school and to enable them to be the very best they can possibly be. Aligning these components will give you many more effective ways to deal with problematic behavior, thus creating and maintaining an environment where everyone does more than just survive; they thrive.

CHAPTER 7 QUESTIONS TO PONDER

1. In looking at the 43 intervention strategies, are there certain ones to which I immediately gravitate because of my own comfort level?
2. Are there some that I might like to entertain if I'm given more guidance?

Table 7.1   Intervention Strategies Described

Strategy	Description
Affirmative Statements	Verbally acknowledge and emphasize the teacher's strengths and achievements.
Appeal to Values	After providing opportunity for self-reflection, discuss concerns and compare them to the positive values the teacher holds as demonstrated in the past.
Ask Closed Questions	Ask questions that can normally be answered using a specific piece of information or a simple "yes" or "no."
Ask Convergent Questions	Ask questions that allow for only very specific acceptable answers.
Ask Open-ended Questions	Ask questions that provide for more than one simple answer, requiring the teacher to think more deeply about the behavior or the attitude.
Ask Self-evaluative Questions	Ask questions that cause the teacher to self-reflect on the behavior.
Ask "What" Questions	Ask "what" questions until the teacher acknowledges the action and volunteers a solution.
Assign a Mentor	Assign the teacher a mentor who demonstrates the desired behavior.
Assisted Goal Setting	Help the teacher set achievable goals to improve behavior in a step-by-step manner.
Brainstorm	Assist the teacher in thinking through alternative approaches to improve the behavior.
Check for Understanding	To avoid the inappropriate behavior, have the teacher paraphrase the instructions, ensuring understanding of your expectations.
Collaborate	Have the teacher work together with others and self-assess how successful their solutions have been at solving the problem.
Confront	Directly address the inappropriate behavior being very specific about what is expected and what is not appropriate.
Directed Change	Provide specific directives with the goal of changing the behavior and thus the results.
Encourage Confidence	Provide positive statements about the teacher's ability to achieve success using examples from previous experiences.
Guided Empathy	Help the teacher appreciate another's situation and to gain a better understanding of how he or she might feel in the same circumstance.
Guided Problem-Solving	Provide opportunities to solve the problem by suggesting possible solutions and allowing the teacher to create alternatives.
Humor	Use humor to lighten a stressful situation.
Increase Physical Presence	Spend more time at the location where the problem behavior appears to be occurring most often.
Individual Accountability	Identify the area of concern and allow the teacher to personally address it.
Manage Anger	Require the teacher to participate in anger management strategies.
Modeling	Demonstrate through example the behavior that is expected of the teacher.
Monitor Closely	Assess the teacher's progress as it relates to the given expectations.

Strategy	Description
Negotiate	Work to reach a compromise with the teacher through open discussion.
Nonverbal Communication	Use eye contact, body movement, or hand signals to gain the teacher's attention.
Orchestrate Positive Peer Reinforcement	Enlist fellow teachers to provide encouragement and affirmation for the teacher having difficulty.
Outside Assistance	Coordinate help from an outside source with the specific skills needed to address the issue.
Persuade	Use reasoning to help the teacher understand the need for change.
Prioritize Concerns	Provide a list of concerns in specific areas that need to be addressed by the teacher.
Provide Alternatives	Provide viable, appropriate options to the current inappropriate behaviors of the teacher.
Provide Conflict Resolution	Help the teacher resolve disputes through discussion and understanding and by jointly developing a resolution.
Provide Feedback	Give a timely assessment regarding what the teacher is doing correctly and what needs to be improved.
Provide Leadership Opportunities	Provide the teacher with opportunities to take on leadership roles related to the area of concern.
Provide a Timeline for Improvement	Provide the teacher with a specific set of objectives for improvement that must be met along with clearly identified dates for attaining those objectives.
Redirect	Stop the teacher's inappropriate behavior and refocus the attention to the task at hand.
Reflect Verbal Responses	Verbally reflect the essence of the teacher's argument in order to clarify his or her true feelings regarding the situation.
Reflective Journaling	Provide a journal for the teacher to reflect on the behavior and determine a more positive course of action in the future.
Reframing	Help the teacher understand the impact of his or her words or actions and the need to consider alternatives.
Review Policies and Procedures	Through verbal or written means, remind the teacher of specific written policies regarding the undesirable behavior.
Self-Disclosure	Allow the teacher an opportunity to personally identify the issue and determine alternatives to resolve the problem.
Suggest Activities	Provide a list of activities the teacher could use as an alternative in the future.
Timely Identification of Inappropriate Behavior	Address the concerning behavior as soon as is reasonably possible in order to stop it from reoccurring.
Written Plan	Develop a clear, concise plan for the teacher that contains specific goals and a timeline for achieving those goals.

Table 7.2   Strategies by Levels of Intrusiveness

Levels of Intrusiveness			
Less ←		→ More	
Encouraging	*Coaching*	*Structuring*	*Directing*
Affirmative Statements	Appeal to Values	Ask Open-ended Questions	Ask Closed Questions
Assign a Mentor	Assisted Goal Setting	Ask Self-evaluative Questions	Ask Convergent Questions
Check for Understanding	Brainstorm	Individual Accountability	Ask "What" Questions
Encourage Confidence	Collaborate	Negotiate	Confront
Humor	Guided Empathy	Orchestrate Positive Peer Reinforcement	Directed Change
Increase Physical Presence	Guided Problem-Solving	Persuade	Manage Anger
Modeling	Monitor Closely	Prioritize Concerns	Outside Assistance
Nonverbal Communication	Provide Leadership Opportunities	Provide Alternatives	Provide Conflict Resolution
Provide Feedback	Reflect Verbal Responses	Provide a Timeline for Improvement	Redirect
Review Policies and Procedures	Reframing	Reflective Journaling	Written Plan
	Self-Disclosure	Suggest Activities	
	Timely Identification of Inappropriate Behavior		

Chapter 8

How to Use the Individualized
Intervention Strategy System

Used in a step-by-step manner (see Table 8.1), the goal of the Individualized Intervention Strategy System (IISS) is to facilitate you, the school leader, in identifying the problem or challenge, determining the stage of motivation and behavior style of the teacher, and selecting the appropriate intervention strategy that might have the highest probability of working. However, we have found that experienced educators learn the prescribed system initially but then later creatively pick and choose strategies based upon the unique challenges of every situation.

To facilitate your use of the IISS, we suggest you first identify the challenge or problematic issue. Second, make a copy of the three pertinent worksheets: the Problem-Solving Worksheet (Figure 8.1), which will serve as your guiding recording document; the Stage of Motivation Checklist (Figure 8.2); and the Behavior Style Checklist (Figure 8.3). Third, complete both of the checklists to determine the individual's Stage of Motivation and Behavior Style and record these results on the Problem-Solving Worksheet. While a teacher's issue may seem quite obvious, to choose an intervention that most effectively meets the needs, you will first refer to the teacher's behavior style. Once determined, go to the appropriate Teacher Improvement Plan that corresponds with the teacher's behavior style: Self-Assertive (Table 8.2), Socially Interactive (Table 8.3), Analytic (Table 8.4), or Accommodating (Table 8.5). On the appropriate table, find the problematic issue from the alphabetical list in the left-hand column. Once found, then refer back to the teacher's stage of motivation: Others Oriented, Relationship Oriented, Approval Oriented, or Self-Absorbed. You will then go across the table where you will find four types of strategies based upon the needed level of intrusiveness: Encouraging (E), Coaching (C), Supporting (S), or Directing (D). Those at Stage 4 typically respond best by using the least intrusive or Encouraging strategies, while those at Stage 1 respond better to those that are more intrusive or Directing. Once you have chosen the appropriate strategy type and have logged it on your Problem-Solving Worksheet, go to the Individualized Intervention Strategies in chapter 9 where the problematic issues are listed alphabetically and are accompanied by step-by-step strategies to assist you in changing the behavior. Feel free to choose the strategy that works best and implement the steps recommended for that particular strategy. Once you have implemented a specific strategy, complete the results section on the Problem-Solving Worksheet where you reflect upon what happened and determine what you'd like to do next.

The terms "practical" and "extremely effective" have been used to describe the conceptual framework and problem-solving system when applied in previous manuals for addressing classroom management (Selig & Arroyo, 1996), character development (Selig, Arroyo, & Tonkin, 2009), and the building of resilient students (Selig, Arroyo, Lloyd-Zannini, & Jordan, 2006). The bottom line is using this system to address multiple short-term problems, while fostering growth and development with the faculty and staff assigned to the school.

Table 8.1   Ten Steps to Enhance Teacher Performance

1. Identify the challenge or problematic issue.
2. Make a copy of the Problem-Solving Worksheet, the Stage of Motivation Checklist, and the Behavior Style Checklist.
3. Complete the Stage of Motivation and the Behavior Style Checklists and record the results on the Problem-Solving Worksheet.
4. Based upon the teacher's Behavior Style (Self-Assertive, Socially Interactive, Analytic, or Accommodating), refer to the appropriate page of the Teacher Improvement Plan.
5. On the appropriate table, find the problematic issue in the alphabetical list.
6. Referring back to the teacher's Stage of Motivation (Others Oriented, Relationship Oriented, Approval Oriented, or Self-Absorbed), go across the table where you will find four types of strategies (Encouraging, Coaching, Structuring, and Directing) based upon the level of intrusiveness needed.
7. Identify the appropriate strategy type and record this on your Problem-Solving Worksheet.
8. Go to the Individualized Intervention Strategies in chapter 9 where each alphabetically listed problem has step-by-step Encouraging, Coaching, Structuring, and Directing strategies to assist you in changing the behavior.
9. Complete the Results section of the Problem-Solving Worksheet where you will reflect upon what happened and what you would like to do next.
10. Remember, the goal is to enhance teacher performance from problematic to good and from good to great!

Problem Solving Worksheet

Teacher's Name: _____R F_____   Date: __6/21/2019__

Problematic Issue: *negativity, lack of collegiality, emotional inappropriate*

Stage of Motivation	Behavior Style			
	Self-Assertive	Socially Interactive	Analytic	Accommodating
Self-Absorbed	✓			
Approval Oriented				
Relationship Oriented				
Others Oriented				

Intervention Strategy: *directing behavior*

Page Number: *pp. 93, 107, 135*

Results:

Anticipated results: angry outburst initially, defensive behavior. after reassurance that she is a valuable asset to the school, hopefully an agreement that the behavior is inappropriate and the desire to work with her teacher colleagues and administration more positively.

Figure 8.1

Stage of Motivation Checklist

Teacher's Name: __RF_____ Date: __6/21/2019__

Stage 1 Self-Absorbed	Stage 2 Approval Oriented	Stage 3 Relationship Oriented	Stage 4 Others Oriented
✓ Usually wants his or her own way	✓ Pursues certain subjects, activities, or hobbies in order to win approval	___ Wants to be respected for his or her ideas	___ Seeks opportunities to help others
___ Has a very short attention span and changes activities often	✓ Seeks attention	___ Loyal, standing up for family or friends	___ Often praises peers, even in their absence
___ Very possessive of his or her belongings	✓ Completes most tasks, but seeks verbal praise for his or her efforts	___ Even tempered and self-controlled	___ Self-motivated and enjoys feeling productive
___ Uses other people's belongings without asking permission	✓ Seeks admiration for his or her achievements	___ Enjoys organized group activities	___ Volunteers for necessary tasks
✓ Becomes angry or resentful if opposed	✓ Enjoys participating in competitive activities, but is upset if his or her efforts go unrecognized	___ Has a healthy appreciation of rules and group norms	___ Makes objective decisions
✓ Gets unusually upset when contradicted	___ Judges others quickly, especially those whose achievements have been recently recognized	___ Strives for competence	___ Converses with peers, administrators, parents, and students on their respective levels
✓ Often must be told specifically what behavior is expected before he or she will comply	✓ Behaves best when he or she is the center of attention	___ Enjoys being part of a particular group	___ Generally optimistic and resilient
✓ Has a low trust level, especially for those in authority	✓ Loses interest in a task if not given constant attention and encouragement	___ Enjoys being associated with a group, organization, or team	___ Stands up for his or her beliefs, even in the face of criticism
___ **Total Checked**	___ **Total Checked**	___ **Total Checked**	___ **Total Checked**

Figure 8.2

Behavior Style Checklist

Teacher's Name: _____RF_____ Date: _6/21/2019_

Instructions
After reviewing the behavior styles, think about a specific setting (e.g., a classroom or in meetings) and check the items below that describe this teacher's typical behavior within that context. Total the checkmarks for each behavior style. The style with the highest number of items checked is the one that best describes this individual in that particular situation.

Self-Assertive	Socially Interactive	Analytic	Accommodating
✓ Outspoken, opinionated, and assertive	___ Uses facial expressions and hand movements when talking	___ Systematic and well-ordered, prefers to have a plan or method	___ Has an honest, low-key style
___ Active and resists staying in one place	___ Expresses himself or herself well verbally	___ Seems very organized	___ Likes routine-is predictable and not quick to change
✓ Persistent-keeps pushing until goal is reached	___ Tends to be cheerful and sees the bright side of situations	___ Seems prepared for most events or activities	___ Seems mild tempered
✓ Decisive - makes decisions easily and sticks with them	___ Persuasive - can present ideas convincingly	___ Tries hard to avoid unwanted surprises	___ Humble and modest about accomplishments
✓ Usually wins arguments or debates	___ Open-minded-open to others' ideas	___ Seeks details	___ Compassionate-tends to be one of the first to help someone who is sick or hurting
✓ Tells people what he or she thinks	___ Friendly and outgoing	___ Keeps records	___ Reserved around new people or in new situations
✓ Gets right to the point	___ Doesn't mind changing plans and is flexible	___ Restrained and usually very self-controlled, seldom loses temper	___ Takes time to think things through and get in touch with his or her feelings
___ Usually takes a leading role in a group	___ Enjoys being around people most of the time	___ Appears to be steady and calm	___ Tenderhearted - usually approaches people in a gentle, soft manner
✓ Productive-works hard and gets a lot done	___ Likes change and diversity	___ Often critical of self	___ Empathetic - considers other people's thoughts and feelings
___ Does not change mind easily once opinion has been formed	___ Highly verbal	___ Prefers to thoroughly understand a new task or situation before trying it	___ Prefers an organized environment with a minimum of unexpected change
✓ Likes to work independently and is able to do so effectively	___ Expresses affection and appreciation for others	___ Approaches most problems in a logical fashion	___ Appears ready to defend and protect others, especially those in a weaker position
✓ Competitive-strives to be first in most things	___ Is original-thinks of new and different ways to do things	___ Usually careful and tactful when communicating with others	___ Stable, acts sensibly and responsibly
✓ Tends to be result oriented	___ Enjoys discussing goals and dreams	___ Thorough, often checking things multiple times	___ Usually calm, easygoing, and relaxed
___ **Total Checked**	___ **Total Checked**	___ **Total Checked**	___ **Total Checked**

Figure 8.3

Table 8.2 Teacher Improvement Plan

	SELF-ASSERTIVE			
	Level of Intrusiveness			
	Less ◄			► More
Problematic Issue	**Stage 4** **Others** **Oriented**	**Stage 3** **Relationship** **Oriented**	**Stage 2** **Approval** **Oriented**	**Stage 1** **Self-Absorbed**
Absenteeism/Tardiness	E	C	S	S
Accountability	C	S	D	D
Arrogance	C	S	D	D
Assessment	E	C	S	S
Blame Shifting	C	S	S	D
Classroom Culture	E	C	S	D
Classroom Management	E	C	S	D
Cliquishness	E	C	S	D
Collegiality	E	C	S	D
Compassion	E	C	C	S
Content Knowledge	E	C	C	S
Critical Thinking Skills	E	E	C	S
Curriculum	E	E	C	S
Disingenuousness	C	S	D	D
Disloyalty	C	S	D	D
Emotional Inappropriateness	E	C	S	D
Exaggeration	E	C	S	S
Feedback	E	C	S	D
Goal Setting	E	C	S	S
Gossip	E	C	S	D
Impulsivity	E	C	S	D
Indifference	E	C	S	D
Inflexibility	C	S	D	D
Initiative	E	C	S	D
Insensitivity	E	C	S	D
Insincerity	E	C	S	S
Instructional Strategies	E	C	C	S
Judgmental	E	C	S	D
Listening	E	C	S	S
Negativity	C	S	S	D
Noncompliance	C	S	D	D
Parent Interaction	C	S	D	D
Planning Skills	E	C	S	S
Resentfulness	C	S	D	D
Self-centeredness	C	S	D	D
Technology	E	E	C	S
Time Management	E	E	C	S
Writing Skills	E	E	C	S

Handwritten margin notes: 5, 10, 15, 20, 25, 30, 35, 38 (line numbers); #3, #2, #1 (arrows). Several "D" and "S" entries in the Stage 1 column are circled.

Table 8.3   Teacher Improvement Plan

	SOCIALLY INTERACTIVE			
	Level of Intrusiveness			
	Less ◄──────────────────────────► More			
Problematic Issue	Stage 4 Others Oriented	Stage 3 Relationship Oriented	Stage 2 Approval Oriented	Stage 1 Self-Absorbed
Absenteeism/Tardiness	E	C	S	S
Accountability	E	C	C	S
Arrogance	E	C	S	D
Assessment	E	C	C	S
Blame Shifting	E	C	S	D
Classroom Culture	E	C	S	S
Classroom Management	E	C	S	S
Cliquishness	E	C	C	S
Collegiality	E	C	C	S
Compassion	E	C	C	S
Content Knowledge	E	C	C	S
Critical Thinking Skills	E	C	C	S
Curriculum	E	C	C	S
Disingenuousness	E	C	S	D
Disloyalty	E	C	S	D
Emotional Inappropriateness	E	C	C	S
Exaggeration	E	C	S	D
Feedback	E	C	C	S
Goal Setting	E	C	C	S
Gossip	E	C	S	D
Impulsivity	E	C	S	S
Indifference	E	C	S	D
Inflexibility	E	C	S	S
Initiative	E	C	C	S
Insensitivity	E	C	C	S
Insincerity	E	C	S	D
Instructional Strategies	E	C	C	S
Judgmental	E	C	C	S
Listening	E	C	C	S
Negativity	E	C	C	S
Noncompliance	E	C	S	D
Parent Interaction	E	C	S	S
Planning Skills	E	C	C	S
Resentfulness	E	C	C	S
Self-centeredness	E	C	C	S
Technology	E	C	C	S
Time Management	E	C	C	S
Writing Skills	E	C	C	S

Table 8.4   Teacher Improvement Plan

Problematic Issue	ANALYTIC			
	Level of Intrusiveness			
	Less ←		→ *More*	
	Stage 4 Others Oriented	Stage 3 Relationship Oriented	Stage 2 Approval Oriented	Stage 1 Self-Absorbed
Absenteeism/Tardiness	E	C	C	S
Accountability	E	E	C	C
Arrogance	E	E	C	S
Assessment	E	E	C	C
Blame Shifting	E	C	C	S
Classroom Culture	E	C	S	S
Classroom Management	E	C	C	S
Cliquishness	E	E	C	S
Collegiality	E	C	C	S
Compassion	E	E	C	C
Content Knowledge	E	E	C	C
Critical Thinking Skills	E	E	C	C
Curriculum	E	E	C	S
Disingenuousness	E	C	S	D
Disloyalty	E	C	S	D
Emotional Inappropriateness	E	C	S	D
Exaggeration	E	C	S	S
Feedback	E	C	S	S
Goal Setting	E	C	C	S
Gossip	E	C	S	D
Impulsivity	E	C	S	S
Indifference	E	C	S	D
Inflexibility	E	C	S	S
Initiative	E	C	S	S
Insensitivity	E	C	C	S
Insincerity	E	C	S	D
Instructional Strategies	E	C	C	S
Judgmental	E	C	S	D
Listening	E	C	C	S
Negativity	E	S	S	D
Noncompliance	E	C	S	D
Parent Interaction	E	C	S	D
Planning Skills	E	C	S	S
Resentfulness	E	C	S	S
Self-centeredness	E	C	S	S
Technology	E	E	S	S
Time Management	E	C	C	S
Writing Skills	E	S	S	S

Table 8.5   Teacher Improvement Plan

	ACCOMMODATING			
	Level of Intrusiveness			
	Less ◄─────────────────────────► More			
Problematic Issue	Stage 4 *Others Oriented*	Stage 3 *Relationship Oriented*	Stage 2 *Approval Oriented*	Stage 1 *Self-Absorbed*
Absenteeism/Tardiness	E	C	C	S
Accountability	E	C	S	S
Arrogance	E	E	C	S
Assessment	E	E	C	C
Blame Shifting	E	C	C	S
Classroom Culture	E	C	S	S
Classroom Management	E	C	C	S
Cliquishness	E	E	C	C
Collegiality	E	E	C	C
Compassion	E	E	E	C
Content Knowledge	E	E	C	S
Critical Thinking Skills	E	C	C	S
Curriculum	E	C	C	S
Disingenuousness	E	C	S	D
Disloyalty	E	C	S	D
Emotional Inappropriateness	E	E	E	S
Exaggeration	E	C	C	S
Feedback	E	E	C	S
Goal Setting	E	E	C	C
Gossip	E	C	C	S
Impulsivity	E	E	C	S
Indifference	E	C	S	S
Inflexibility	E	E	C	C
Initiative	E	C	C	S
Insensitivity	E	E	C	C
Insincerity	E	E	C	C
Instructional Strategies	E	E	C	C
Judgmental	E	C	C	S
Listening	E	E	E	C
Negativity	E	C	C	S
Noncompliance	E	C	S	D
Parent Interaction	E	C	C	S
Planning Skills	E	C	C	S
Resentfulness	E	C	C	S
Self-centeredness	E	C	C	S
Technology	E	C	C	S
Time Management	E	E	C	S
Writing Skills	E	E	C	S

Chapter 9

Individualized Intervention Strategies

Containing over 300 individualized intervention strategies, this chapter is by far the lengthiest in the book. Listed alphabetically, within each of the 38 problematic issues, you will find step-by-step strategies based upon the four Stages of Motivation.

Beginning with the teacher's determined stage of motivation is simply a starting point for you to begin your intervention. You will find that some strategies work better for some individuals, but feel free to change strategies as the need requires. We encourage you to look at other strategies that might work even though we don't usually show them at the particular stage you are dealing with. The purpose is to provide you with a multitude of strategies that have proven effective over the years and the key is for you to be flexible enough to use the one that works regardless of whether we recommend it or not.

ABSENTEEISM/TARDINESS

Encouraging

Intervention Strategies

➤ **Increase Physical Presence**
   Spend more time at the location where the problem behavior appears to occur most often.
   1. Arrange to be present in situations where the teacher's absence or tardiness typically occurs.
   2. At critical times, position yourself near the locations where the teacher is assigned but may not be fulfilling duties.
   3. Frequently visit the classroom of the teacher who may not be where and when he or she should be.
   4. In the strategies above, verbal communication is usually not needed; your physical proximity and presence is often enough to change the behavior.

➤ **Nonverbal Communication**
   Use eye contact, body movement, or hand signals to gain the teacher's attention.
   1. Physically acknowledge tardiness via a look at the clock, a facial expression, or some other appropriate body language.
   2. Create a sense of community, respect, and care through nonverbal communication exhibiting your pleasure at seeing the teacher neither absent nor tardy.
   3. Physically acknowledge attendance/promptness via a smile, a nod of approval, or a thumbs-up.

ABSENTEEISM/TARDINESS

Coaching

Intervention Strategies

➤ **Assisted Goal Setting**
   Help the teacher set achievable goals to improve behavior in a step-by-step manner.
   1. Reinforce the need for teachers to be both present and prompt for work.
   2. Collaboratively brainstorm specific and realistic goals in which the teacher can slowly begin to implement better and more timely attendance strategies.
   3. Establish benchmarks to monitor progress.
   4. Providing feedback; periodically follow up with the teacher to ensure compliance and establish new goals if necessary.

➤ **Monitor Closely**
   Assess the teacher's progress as it relates to the given expectations.
   1. Determine the teacher's current perception of the situation.
   2. Remind the teacher of the attendance/promptness expectations ensuring the teacher understands their importance.
   3. Ask the teacher to consider the situation from a different vantage point and if he or she is unable to do this, share an example.
   4. Encourage the teacher to verbalize some possible options as to how better attendance or more prompt behavior can best be accomplished.
   5. Monitor the teacher closely to see if attendance/promptness improves.

ABSENTEEISM/TARDINESS

Structuring

Intervention Strategies

➢ **Ask Open-ended Questions**

Ask questions that provide for more than one simple answer, requiring the teacher to think more deeply about the behavior.

1. When trying to determine the reason behind the frequent absences or tardiness, ask questions such as "Is there anything going on with you that's causing you to be absent/late so often?"
2. Ask "What effect do you think your absence or tardiness has on _____?"
3. Ask the teacher what he or she could do in the future to improve attendance or timeliness.
4. Establish a verbal agreement with the teacher to be present and on time.
5. Monitor progress to determine if attendance/promptness improves or if greater intervention is necessary.

➢ **Provide a Timeline for Improvement**

Provide the teacher with a specific set of objectives for improvement that must be met along with clearly identified dates for attaining those objectives.

1. Review the requirements for attendance/promptness at work with the teacher.
2. Agree upon a timeline for improvement.
3. Implement monitoring procedures such as having the teacher sign in at the office for the next month until attendance/tardiness improves.
4. Follow up to ensure compliance, providing positive feedback as improvement is noted.

ABSENTEEISM/TARDINESS

Directing

Intervention Strategies

➢ **Confront**

Directly address the inappropriate behavior being very specific about what is expected and what is not appropriate.

1. State specifically what the continuous attendance/promptness issues are.
2. Review steps needed to improve attendance/promptness.
3. While providing the teacher an opportunity to respond, reiterate the problem and how it must be corrected immediately.
4. Closely monitor the teacher's progress toward the stated expectations and take alternative actions as necessary.

➢ **Directed Change**

Provide specific directives with the goal of changing the behavior and thus the results.

1. Identify the specific issues with attendance/tardiness, providing specific dates and times of the infractions.
2. Discuss with the teacher reasons why he or she needs to be present and on time (e.g., student safety, improved learning, contractual obligations).
3. Provide a specific plan for improvement such as providing doctor's notes for absences or signing in at the office each day.
4. Identify specific consequences for not following the plan such as docking personal leave or pay.
5. Follow up to ensure compliance.

ACCOUNTABILITY

Encouraging

Intervention Strategies

➢ **Encourage Confidence**
Provide positive statements about the teacher's ability to achieve success using examples from previous experiences.
1. Through faculty meetings or other faculty communications, remind teachers of the need to be accountable.
2. Make time to visit the teacher who seems to be falling short on accountability and express your confidence in his or her ability to comply with the expectations.
3. When expectations are being met, be quick to affirm and applaud the teacher's efforts.

➢ **Review Policies and Procedures**
Through verbal or written means, remind the teacher of specific written policies regarding the undesirable behavior.
1. Periodically remind everyone of personal accountability principles teachers are expected to follow.
2. In faculty and staff communications, highlight a variety of exemplary personal accountability examples.
3. Make an effort to personally encourage teachers who may have been struggling with accountability when they have done a good job.

ACCOUNTABILITY

Coaching

Intervention Strategies

➢ **Guided Problem-Solving**
Provide opportunities to solve the problem by suggesting possible solutions and allowing the teacher to create alternatives.
1. Identify specific areas in which accountability issues need to be addressed by the teacher.
2. Prioritize the areas of accountability that need attention.
3. Collaboratively generate strategies that will assist the teacher in addressing these areas of need.
4. Provide encouragement to the teacher when you see evidence of increased accountability.

➢ **Provide Leadership Opportunities**
Provide the teacher with opportunities to take on leadership roles related to the area of concern.
1. In areas of strength, assign the teacher to leadership positions on committees.
2. Coach the teacher in his or her leadership capacity and collaboratively strategize about leading effective team meetings.
3. Meet periodically to encourage the teacher's accountability as a leader, particularly focusing on statements or actions that demonstrate responsibility.

ACCOUNTABILITY

Structuring

Intervention Strategies

➢ **Ask Self-Evaluative Questions**
Ask questions that cause the teacher to self-reflect on the behavior.
1. When you see the teacher not meeting his or her responsibilities, inquire as to what is happening, while trying to determine the root cause of the lack of accountability.
2. Ask the teacher to self-evaluate and articulate the reasons why he or she is failing to meet expectations in the particular problematic area.
3. Compare the teacher's self-evaluation with your perceptions and together determine a plan for improvement.

➢ **Prioritize Concerns**
Provide a list of concerns in specific areas that need to be addressed by the teacher.
1. Meet with the teacher to identify and analyze the areas that fall short in terms of student achievement.
2. Determine what areas of student success need to be addressed first.
3. Collaboratively generate strategies that will assist the teacher in accepting responsibility for student success.
4. Check back frequently on the progress and make adjustments as needed.

ACCOUNTABILITY

Directing

Intervention Strategies

➢ **Ask Convergent Questions**
Ask questions that allow for very specific acceptable answers.
1. Ask the teacher to explain his or her understanding of the policy regarding the expectation for teachers to be accountable for (area of concern).
2. Ask the teacher to compare his or her understanding with the written expectations that have been provided.
3. Ask if the teacher understands the policy as written and what he or she sees is needed to bring compliance.
4. If necessary, provide specific directives as to what he or she must do to be in alignment with the policies or procedures.

➢ **Confront**
Directly address the inappropriate behavior being very specific about what is expected and what is not appropriate.
1. Ask the teacher to explain his or her reason for the lack of accountability.
2. Ask the teacher if there are ways to improve his or her accountability. If the teacher identifies new strategies, provide the support needed to implement them and if none are identified, provide alternatives you would like to see used.
3. Have the teacher articulate what he or she will do the next time.
4. Monitor the teacher regularly to ensure implementation.

ARROGANCE

Encouraging

Intervention Strategies

➤ **Nonverbal Communication**
  Use eye contact, body movement, or hand signals to gain the teacher's attention.
  1. Physically acknowledge arrogance via a facial expression such as a raised eyebrow or some other appropriate body language. If the problem persists, verbally confer with the teacher.
  2. Make an effort to frequently be in areas where the teacher is interacting with others and then purposely acknowledge in a more humble manner by smiling, nodding, or gesturing a signal of satisfaction, like a thumbs-up.
  3. Keep a written record of the positive interactions you can share with the teacher on a regular basis.

➤ **Provide Feedback**
  Give a timely assessment regarding what the teacher is doing correctly and what needs to be improved.
  1. Verbally give a specific description of how the teacher manifested an arrogant attitude in a particular situation and how it affected others.
  2. Ask the teacher if there are alternative ways to interact that would not be perceived as arrogant.
  3. Provide specific alternatives as necessary.
  4. Monitor the teacher's interactions and be ready to praise improvement.

ARROGANCE

Coaching

Intervention Strategies

➤ **Appeal to Values**
  Providing opportunity for self-reflection, discuss concerns and compare them to the positive values the teacher holds as demonstrated in the past.
  1. Gently remind the teacher of what he or she holds dear in terms of value.
  2. Inquire if the teacher thinks arrogance is appropriate.
  3. Have the teacher think about his or her attitude and identify a more appropriate response.
  4. Praise positive responses, and if there is a lapse in appropriate behavior, compare the reaction to the teacher's more typical positive behavior.

➤ **Timely Identification of Inappropriate Behavior**
  Address the concerning behavior as soon as is reasonably possible in order to stop it from reoccurring.
  1. Facilitate trust through regular, timely, and open interaction.
  2. When the teacher displays arrogant behavior, privately bring it to his or her attention as soon as possible.
  3. Remind the teacher of possible alternative responses that have been previously discussed.
  4. Be quick to acknowledge and affirm appropriate responses until arrogance is significantly reduced.

ARROGANCE

Structuring

Intervention Strategies

➢ **Persuade**

Use reasoning to help the teacher understand the need for change.

1. Affirm your esteem for the teacher as part of the school and point out positive contributions.
2. State your specific concerns about the teacher's arrogant behavior or attitude.
3. Offer possible alternatives to the current behavior or attitude that would result in better relationships.
4. Continue the discussion until you have persuaded the teacher that a less arrogant attitude is more acceptable.
5. Follow up with the teacher to ensure the attitude is improving.

➢ **Reflective Journaling**

Provide a journal for the teacher to reflect on the behavior and determine a more positive course of action in the future.

1. Discuss with the teacher the perceived arrogance.
2. Ask the teacher to log his or her interactions with others and note where arrogance might have surfaced.
3. In those incidents where the teacher believes the response may have been anything other than humble, have him or her reflect on ways the situation could have been handled better.
4. Have the teacher leave a margin on the right-hand side of the journal page for you to respond to the journal entry.
5. If the reflection is rather shallow, elicit additional thoughts and feelings in a nondirective manner until the desired level of understanding of the arrogance is reached. This could be done in writing through the journal or in person.
6. Conclude interactions with encouragement and affirmation.

ARROGANCE

Directing

Intervention Strategies

➢ **Ask "What" Questions**

Ask "what" questions until the teacher acknowledges the action and volunteers a solution.

1. When trying to determine the reason behind the arrogant attitude/behavior, ask questions such as "What makes you think your way is the right way?"
2. Ask "What do you think (name of person) could contribute to the conversation?"
3. Follow up by asking other questions such as "What could you have done differently?"
4. Establish a verbal agreement with the teacher that he or she will begin taking ownership of the attitude/behavior and attempt to make changes.
5. Monitor the teacher's attitude/behavior to determine if it improves or if greater intervention is necessary.

➢ **Provide Conflict Resolution**

Help the teacher resolve disputes through discussion and understanding and by jointly developing a resolution.

1. Identify the conflict caused by the teacher's perceived arrogance.
2. Describe the impact the arrogance has on others.
3. Ask the teacher to describe his or her understanding of the issue.
4. Suggest ways the arrogant attitude can be diminished or eliminated.
5. Stay with the process until there has been acknowledgment of the arrogance and the conflict diminishes.
6. Arrange to revisit the situation in a timely fashion to monitor progress.

ASSESSMENT

Encouraging

Intervention Strategies

➢ **Check for Understanding**
To avoid the inappropriate behavior, have the teacher paraphrase the instructions ensuring understanding of your expectations.
1. In your discussions regarding assessing students, frequently ask the teacher questions to discern his or her level of knowledge regarding varied assessments.
2. In areas that seem unclear to the teacher, explain how to effectively use a variety of assessments to gauge student learning.
3. Have the teacher explain to you his or her understanding of what was explained.
4. After the teacher has tried varied assessments, have him or her share with you what was learned from the experience and how it might be improved the next time.

➢ **Review Policies and Procedures**
Through verbal or written means, remind the teacher of specific written policies regarding the undesirable behavior.
1. At strategic faculty meetings, highlight the assessment policies and procedures of both the school and the district.
2. Through various faculty and staff communications, highlight a variety of different assessment strategies that teachers are encouraged to use.
3. Encourage the teacher to begin with the end (i.e., assessment) in mind and to use backward design when planning lessons.

ASSESSMENT

Coaching

Intervention Strategies

➢ **Assisted Goal Setting**
Help the teacher set achievable goals to improve behavior in a step-by-step manner.
1. Reinforce the need to develop assessment goals to improve student learning.
2. Collaboratively brainstorm specific and realistic goals the teacher can slowly begin to implement into his or her classes.
3. Establish benchmarks to monitor progress.
4. Provide feedback by periodically following up with the teacher to ensure compliance and establish new goals as necessary.

➢ **Monitor Closely**
Assess the teacher's progress as it relates to the given expectations.
1. Determine the teacher's current perception of his or her student assessment practices.
2. Ask the teacher if he or she is using a variety of strategies and when the last time he or she used _____? (Name one you know has been missing).
3. Encourage the teacher to verbalize some possible options as to what strategy to try next.
4. Monitor the teacher closely to see if frequent praise of new strategy implementation elicits the desired change.

ASSESSMENT

Structuring

Intervention Strategies

> **Prioritize Concerns**
>
> *Provide a list of concerns in specific areas that need to be addressed by the teacher.*
> 1. Meet with the teacher to identify and analyze the students' assessment needs.
> 2. Identify specific areas in which student assessment needs to be taught by the teacher.
> 3. Determine what areas of student assessment need to be addressed first.
> 4. Collaboratively generate strategies that will assist the teacher in teaching for assessment.
> 5. Check back frequently on the progress and make adjustments as needed.

> **Provide a Timeline for Improvement**
>
> *Provide the teacher with a specific set of objectives for improvement that must be met along with clearly identified dates for attaining those objectives.*
> 1. Identify specific areas in which the teacher is not addressing assessment effectively.
> 2. Discuss how the teacher can teach with assessment in mind.
> 3. Together with the teacher, choose some appropriate assessment strategies and determine when and how they are to be used.
> 4. Agree upon a timeline for improvement and follow up on a scheduled basis to ensure implementation.

ASSESSMENT

Directing

Intervention Strategies

> **Outside Assistance**
>
> *Coordinate help from an outside source with the specific skills needed to help address the issue.*
> 1. Keep an accurate record of the specific problems you have observed related to student assessment and identify outside resources to best assist the teacher.
> 2. Meet with the teacher to discuss your assessment concerns and let him or her know of your intention to provide assistance.
> 3. Bring in outside assistance, discuss your concerns and projected goals, collectively determine the best strategy to approach the situation, and permit that person to work with the teacher.
> 4. Have the outside resource keep in touch with you to be sure that all are on the same page.
> 5. Follow up with the teacher to ensure that he or she is implementing the proper assessment procedures.

> **Written Plan**
>
> *Develop a clear, concise plan for the teacher that contains specific goals and a timeline for achieving those goals.*
> 1. Discuss with the teacher the most appropriate methods for assessing student learning.
> 2. Establish a systematic plan for improving the teacher's assessment methods.
> 3. Sign a written agreement with the teacher that contains a specific timeline for implementation.
> 4. Monitor and revise the plan as necessary.

BLAME SHIFTING

Encouraging

Intervention Strategies

➤ **Check for Understanding**
To avoid the inappropriate behavior, have the teacher paraphrase the instructions ensuring understanding of your expectations.
1. Ask the teacher questions to ascertain if blaming did occur and if that was the intention.
2. Call attention to the need for the teacher to solve the problem, not to place blame.
3. Ask the teacher to determine a more appropriate way to react to the situation accepting responsibility for the attitude and/or behavior.

➤ **Humor**
Use humor to lighten a stressful situation.
1. Establish rapport and relationship with the teacher through appropriate humor, being careful to never be cutting or sarcastic.
2. Find ways to poke fun at yourself to demonstrate similar errors you personally have made in the past and how it was not productive.
3. Send a clear message that, although you are using humor to lighten the mood, you are confident the teacher *can* accept responsibility for his or her own behavior and/or attitude.

BLAME SHIFTING

Coaching

Intervention Strategies

➤ **Reflect Verbal Responses**
Verbally reflect the essence of the teacher's argument in order to clarify his or her true feelings regarding the situation.
1. In order to get the teacher to clarify any underlying meaning, ask him or her, "If I hear you correctly, you are saying _____."
2. Listen carefully to the teacher's response and attempt to understand the underlying meaning.
3. Repeat the message back to the teacher and continue to seek clarity until he or she owns and acknowledges the blame shifting.
4. Ask the teacher what steps can be taken to ensure that blame shifting does not continue to occur.

➤ **Reframing**
Help the teacher understand the impact of his or her words or actions and the need to consider alternatives.
1. Help the teacher understand that blaming others does not solve problems, but instead often exacerbates them while being destructive.
2. Help the teacher understand the impact of what was said and how reframing can accomplish the same goal in a more productive way.
3. Work with the teacher to help him or her learn to reframe statements, removing judgment or condemnation. For example, help the teacher reframe an insensitive statement and rephrase it, eliminating harshness and instead producing kindness.

BLAME SHIFTING

Structuring

Intervention Strategies

➢ **Ask Open-ended Questions**
   Ask questions that provide for more than one simple answer, requiring the teacher to think more deeply about the behavior.
   1. Ask questions such as "What happened? How did you react and what was the response of the other person? Why do you believe it was the other person's fault?" or "Was there any part of the situation that could have been your responsibility?"
   2. Listen carefully and do not formulate the next question until you have paid attention to the response for the first.
   3. Encourage specific and relevant responses with appropriate follow-up questions such as "What could you have done differently?" and "How will you respond differently next time?"

➢ **Provide Alternatives**
   Provide viable, appropriate options to the current inappropriate behaviors of the teacher.
   1. Collaboratively brainstorm realistic and specific alternative reactions to situations as they arise.
   2. Help the teacher determine which alternative reaction to blame shifting might be more appropriate.
   3. Encourage the teacher to begin accepting personal responsibility and pondering different alternative reactions.
   4. Have the teacher regularly touch base with you to discuss specific situations, how he or she reacted to them, and the results that followed.

BLAME SHIFTING

Directing

Intervention Strategies

➢ **Ask "What" Questions**
   Ask "what" questions until the teacher acknowledges the action and volunteers a solution.
   1. When trying to determine the reason behind the frequent blame shifting, ask questions such as "What makes you think it was someone else's fault?"
   2. Ask "What did you say or do?" until the teacher stops making excuses for the behavior and/or attitude and tells you what he or she did.
   3. Follow up by asking other questions such as "What could you have done differently?"
   4. Establish a verbal agreement with the teacher that he or she will begin taking ownership of the behavior.
   5. Monitor the teacher's attitude/behavior to determine if it improves or if greater intervention is necessary.

➢ **Provide Conflict Resolution**
   Help the teacher resolve disputes through discussion and understanding and by jointly developing a resolution.
   1. Encourage open dialogue in an attempt to have the teacher accept responsibility for his or her own behavior or attitude.
   2. Ask the teacher to explain his or her response to the behavior of others.
   3. Ask the teacher if there was a better way he or she could have handled the situation. If the teacher identifies new strategies, provide the support needed to implement them and if none are identified, provide alternatives you would like to see used.
   4. Have the teacher articulate what he or she will do the next time to accept responsibility.
   5. Monitor the teacher's interaction with others affirming the response if appropriate or continuing to provide alternative actions if necessary.

CLASSROOM CULTURE

Encouraging

Intervention Strategies

➤ **Affirmative Statements**
Verbally acknowledge and emphasize the teacher's strengths and achievements.
1. In faculty meetings and other faculty communications, continually praise and encourage positive classroom culture that captivates and engages students.
2. Remind the teacher of past accomplishments and successes that have resulted in a positive classroom environment and encourage him or her to continue to implement these.
3. Praise the teacher when you notice specific things that contribute to a positive classroom environment.

➤ **Assign a Mentor**
Assign the teacher a mentor who demonstrates the desired behavior.
1. Pair the teacher with a role model who excels in creating a positive classroom culture.
2. Have the mentor and teacher collaboratively set goals for improving classroom climate.
3. Check back frequently to monitor progress and make adjustments as needed.

CLASSROOM CULTURE

Coaching

Intervention Strategies

➤ **Collaborate**
Have the teacher work together with others and self-assess how successful their solutions have been at solving the problem.
1. With the help of the teacher, clearly identify the perceived negative classroom culture.
2. Suggest that the teacher having difficulty partner with a colleague within the building who displays exemplary classroom culture.
3. Ask the teacher to work with that partner to generate a list of resources that could assist him or her develop a more positive classroom culture.
4. Categorize the list into resources with which the teacher may feel comfortable and those he or she is not.
5. Have the teacher select two to three resources to assist with improving the classroom environment.
6. After the teacher has made use of the selected resources, plan a classroom visit to check on their effectiveness and provide encouragement where necessary.

➤ **Reflect Verbal Responses**
Verbally reflect the essence of a teacher's argument in order to clarify his or her true feelings regarding the situation.
1. In order to get the teacher to clarify underlying meaning, ask him or her, "If I hear you correctly, you are saying _____."
2. Listen carefully to the teacher's response and attempt to understand the underlying meaning.
3. Repeat the message back to the teacher and continue to seek clarity until ownership of the negative culture is acknowledged.
4. Ask the teacher what steps can be taken to ensure a more positive classroom culture.

CLASSROOM CULTURE

Structuring

Intervention Strategies

➤ **Ask Open-ended Questions**
Ask questions that provide for more than one simple answer, requiring the teacher to think more deeply about the behavior.
1. When trying to determine why the teacher has a negative classroom culture, ask questions such as "What do you think is causing your classroom to have a negative culture?"
2. Follow up by asking "how" questions such as "How do you think the negative classroom culture affects student learning?"
3. Ask another "what" question such as "What do you plan to do to improve your classroom culture?"
4. Establish a verbal agreement with the teacher to improve the classroom culture.
5. Monitor the teacher's classroom to determine if the culture improves or if greater intervention is necessary.

➤ **Provide a Timeline for Improvement**
Provide the teacher with a specific set of objectives for improvement that must be met along with clearly identified dates for attaining those objectives.
1. Define the characteristics of a positive classroom culture and compare those to the culture that has been observed.
2. Collaboratively develop specific and realistic objectives the teacher can use to change the negative classroom environment.
3. Agree upon a timeframe in which these objectives will be implemented.
4. Provide feedback and periodically follow up with the teacher to ensure a more positive culture and establish new objectives if necessary.

CLASSROOM CULTURE

Directing

Intervention Strategies

➤ **Outside Assistance**
Coordinate help from an outside source with the specific skills needed to address the issue.
1. Keep an accurate record of the specific problems you have observed related to negative classroom culture and identify outside resources to best assist the teacher.
2. Meet with the teacher to discuss your concerns about the classroom culture and let him or her know of your intention to provide assistance.
3. Bring in the outside assistance, discuss your concerns and projected goals, collectively determine the best strategy to approach the situation, and permit him or her to work with the teacher.
4. Have the outside resource keep in touch with you to be sure that all are on the same page.
5. Follow up with the teacher to ensure that he or she is implementing the proper procedures to improve the classroom culture.

➤ **Written Plan**
Develop a clear, concise plan for the teacher that contains specific goals and a timeline for achieving those goals.
1. Discuss with the teacher the most appropriate methods for maintaining a positive classroom culture.
2. Establish a systematic plan for improving the teacher's classroom culture.
3. Sign a written agreement with the teacher that contains a specific timeline for implementation.
4. Monitor and revise the plan as necessary.

CLASSROOM MANAGEMENT

Encouraging

Intervention Strategies

➢ **Modeling**
Demonstrate through example the behavior that is expected of the teacher.
1. Frequently acknowledge and praise good classroom management practices you have seen that teachers should emulate.
2. Consider modeling a lesson to demonstrate classroom management strategies that the teacher is not currently using.
3. Be quick to praise the teacher when appropriate classroom management skills are demonstrated.
4. Be consistent in your praise as the teacher demonstrates effective classroom management strategies.

➢ **Review Policies and Procedures**
Through verbal or written means, remind the teacher of specific written policies regarding the undesirable behavior.
1. At strategic faculty meetings, highlight classroom management policies and procedures of both the school and the district.
2. Encourage the teacher to think beyond the immediate to see the long-term benefits of effective classroom management.
3. Make an effort to personally encourage teachers who may have been struggling with classroom management when they have done a good job.

CLASSROOM MANAGEMENT

Coaching

Intervention Strategies

➢ **Brainstorm**
Assist the teacher in thinking through alternative approaches to improve the behavior.
1. Collaboratively brainstorm realistic and specific alternatives to various discipline issues that might arise.
2. Help the teacher determine when to use alternative classroom management procedures.
3. Encourage the teacher to try different alternatives.
4. Have the teacher regularly touch base with you to discuss specific discipline situations, how they were handled, and the results that followed.

➢ **Collaborate**
Have the teacher work together with others and self-assess how successful their solutions have been at solving the problem.
1. Divide the teachers into teams and have them collaboratively develop effective classroom management strategies and present them to one another at a faculty meeting or on an in-service day.
2. Suggest that the teacher having difficulty partner with a colleague within the building who displays exemplary classroom management skills.
3. Provide opportunities for the teacher to observe others who have demonstrated excellence in classroom management at other schools and tie this into recertification points if possible for both the observer and the observed.
4. Bring in outside consultants to provide in-services on effective classroom management strategies as needed.

CLASSROOM MANAGEMENT

Structuring

Intervention Strategies

➤ **Individual Accountability**
Identify the area of concern and allow the teacher to personally address it.
1. Speak to the teacher privately to avoid drawing undue attention to his or her perceived lack of classroom management skills, informing the teacher as to what you have observed.
2. Ask the teacher what areas of classroom management need the greatest support.
3. If necessary, provide possible classroom management suggestions for the teacher until an appropriate response is produced.
4. Affirm the teacher's effort to try new alternatives and express your confidence as improvement is noted.

➤ **Provide a Timeline for Improvement**
Provide the teacher with a specific set of objectives for improvement that must be met along with clearly identified dates for attaining those objectives.
1. Collaboratively brainstorm specific and realistic objectives in which the teacher can change his or her classroom management skills.
2. Agree upon a time frame in which these objectives and goals can be implemented.
3. Provide feedback and periodically follow up with the teacher to ensure improvement and establish new goals if necessary.

CLASSROOM MANAGEMENT

Directing

Intervention Strategies

➤ **Confront**
Directly address the inappropriate behavior being very specific about what is expected and what is not appropriate.
1. State specifically what the continuous classroom management issue is.
2. Review steps needed to improve classroom management.
3. While providing the teacher an opportunity to respond, reiterate the problem and how it must be corrected immediately for the safety of all students.
4. Closely monitor the teacher's progress toward the stated expectations and take alternative actions as necessary.

➤ **Outside Assistance**
Coordinate help from an outside source with the specific skills needed to address the issue.
1. Keep an accurate record of the specific classroom management problem you have observed and identify which outside resource would best assist the teacher.
2. Meet with the teacher to discuss your classroom management concerns and let him or her know of your intention to provide assistance.
3. Develop options for the outside assistance. It may include seminars on classroom management or bringing in consultants or coaches. Discuss your concerns and projected goals with the teacher and collectively determine the best option to approach the situation.
4. Have the outside resource keep in touch with you to be sure that all are on the same page.
5. Follow up with the teacher to ensure that he or she is working to improve the classroom management skills as expected.

CLIQUISHNESS

Encouraging

Intervention Strategies

➤ **Check for Understanding**
To avoid the inappropriate behavior, have the teacher paraphrase the instructions ensuring understanding of your expectations.
1. Provide an opportunity for self-reflection regarding the perceived cliquishness.
2. Inquire if the teacher thinks a climate of cliquishness is appropriate for the setting.
3. Have the teacher describe what he or she believes a more inclusive environment would look like.
4. Develop a plan with the teacher to modify or change the perceived cliquishness.

➤ **Provide Feedback**
Give a timely assessment regarding what the teacher is doing correctly and what needs to be improved.
1. Speak privately to the teacher to avoid drawing undue attention to his or her cliquish tendencies.
2. Ask the teacher what could be done differently and provide appropriate suggestions where necessary.
3. If needed, coach the teacher until an appropriate response is produced.
4. Verbally acknowledge and praise positive changes toward more collaborative behavior.
5. Be consistent in your praise until the teacher internalizes the desired qualities.
6. Praise the teacher's effort to be more inclusive of others and express your confidence as improvement is noted.

CLIQUISHNESS

Coaching

Intervention Strategies

➤ **Guided Problem-Solving**
Provide opportunities to solve the problem by suggesting possible solutions and allowing the teacher to create alternatives.
1. Identify the specific cliquishness observed.
2. Collaborate with the teacher to define the problem in specific terms and evaluate alternative strategies.
3. Guide the teacher to see why it is critical to model healthy interpersonal relationships.
4. Ask the teacher to brainstorm possible strategies that will enable him or her to have a more inclusive mind-set with regard to interpersonal interactions.
5. Provide encouragement and affirmation when you see evidence of more inclusive behavior.

➤ **Monitor Closely**
Assess the teacher's progress as it relates to the given expectations.
1. Determine the teacher's current perception of the situation.
2. Ask the teacher to consider the situation from a different vantage point and if he or she is unable to do this, share an example.
3. Encourage the teacher to verbalize some possible options on how he or she could be less cliquish.
4. Monitor the teacher closely to see if frequent praise of more appropriate interpersonal behavior elicits the desired change.

CLIQUISHNESS

Structuring

Intervention Strategies

➤ **Ask Self-evaluative Questions**
Ask questions that cause the teacher to self-reflect on the behavior.
1. Ask self-evaluative questions that would help the teacher identify the perceived cliquishness in his or her current pattern of relationship.
2. Look for opportunities to ask the teacher how he or she might feel if the incident or issue happened to them.
3. Assist the teacher in determining some ways to diminish the cliquishness so others will feel more part of the group.
4. Encourage the teacher to implement one or more of the solutions to resolve the perceived cliquishness.
5. Provide positive reinforcement when a positive response is elicited and gentle guidance of other alternatives if a negative response is received.

➤ **Provide Alternatives**
Provide viable, appropriate options to the current inappropriate behaviors of the teacher.
1. Collaboratively brainstorm realistic and specific alternatives to potential cliquish situations before they arise.
2. Help the teacher determine which alternative might be more appropriate.
3. Provide the teacher a timeline for trying the different alternatives.
4. Have the teacher regularly touch base with you to discuss specific situations, how they were handled, and the results that followed.
5. If the initial results are not successful in reducing the cliquishness, repeat the process with the teacher.

CLIQUISHNESS

Directing

Intervention Strategies

➤ **Ask Closed Questions**
Ask questions that can normally be answered using a specific piece of information or a simple "yes" or "no."
1. Ask the teacher to respond to a direct question related to the problem such as "Are you including (teacher name) in your collaborative planning group?"
2. Ask the teacher if the perceived cliquish behavior is in the best interest of others or the school and explain why it cannot be tolerated.
3. Express your expectations of who needs to be included in the teacher's collaborative planning groups.
4. Follow up to ensure the teacher is being more inclusive.

➤ **Redirect**
Stop the teacher's inappropriate behavior and refocus the attention to the task at hand.
1. Determine the cause of the cliquishness and explain to the teacher why it is inappropriate.
2. Call the teacher's attention to what he or she is doing that isolates others.
3. Refocus the teacher's attention to positive behavior that contributes to appropriate interpersonal relationships.
4. Clearly identify for the teacher what is expected.
5. Monitor the teacher and praise as needed, elaborating on the positive elements of the new attitude/behavior.

COLLEGIALITY

Encouraging

Intervention Strategies

➢ **Check for Understanding**
   To avoid the inappropriate behavior, have the teacher paraphrase the instructions ensuring understanding of your expectations.
   1. Ask questions to ascertain if the teacher really means to be noncollegial.
   2. Call attention to the need for all teachers to band together in an effort to advance student learning.
   3. Ask the teacher to determine how he or she can interact in a more collegial manner.
   4. Collegially work with the teacher to determine how he or she can work in a more interconnected manner.
   5. Follow up to ensure changes have occurred.

➢ **Modeling**
   Demonstrate through example the behavior that is expected of the teacher.
   1. Model appropriate collegiality.
   2. Verbally acknowledge and praise collegiality in others so the teacher can be reminded of what is expected.
   3. Be quick to praise the teacher when he or she demonstrates appropriate collegiality.
   4. Be consistent in your praise until the teacher internalizes the desired qualities.
   5. Look for opportunities to reinforce that "we are in this together."

COLLEGIALITY

Coaching

Intervention Strategies

➢ **Guided Empathy**
   Help the teacher appreciate another's situation and to gain a better understanding of how he or she might feel in the same circumstance.
   1. Position yourself near the teacher and as appropriate, engage in conversation that focuses on how others might feel, particularly if someone is new or might be feeling left out.
   2. Ask the teacher to "befriend" that individual and see if he or she can offer any assistance.
   3. Be quick to praise the teacher when appropriate responses to others are demonstrated.
   4. Be consistent in your praise until the teacher internalizes the desired qualities.

➢ **Provide Leadership Opportunities**
   Provide the teacher with opportunities to take on leadership roles related to the area of concern.
   1. Give the teacher leadership responsibilities such as acting as a mentor to a new teacher.
   2. Coach the teacher in his or her leadership capacity and strategize with him or her about leading effective team meetings that include others.
   3. Meet periodically to encourage the teacher's leadership skills and to particularly praise collegiality and teamwork.

COLLEGIALITY

Structuring

Intervention Strategies

➤ **Orchestrate Positive Peer Reinforcement**
Enlist fellow teachers to provide encouragement and affirmation for the teacher having difficulty.
1. Discuss with the teacher the issue of collegiality and how it is affecting others.
2. Indicate that you'll be enlisting peers to encourage and affirm the teacher when he or she demonstrates collegial behavior.
3. Select peers to encourage and work with the teacher.
4. Follow up frequently with peers and the teacher to ensure that more cooperative behavior is occurring.

➤ **Suggest Activities**
Provide a list of activities the teacher could use as an alternative in the future.
1. Suggest that the teacher partner with a colleague who displays exemplary collegiality.
2. Divide the teachers into teams and have them collaboratively work together on various projects and present them to one another at a faculty meeting or on an in-service day. Have the teacher who lacks collegiality be the leader of the team.
3. Provide opportunities for the teacher to visit other schools to observe selected teachers with demonstrated excellence in working together with others and tie this into recertification points if possible for both the observed and the observer.
4. Bring in outside consultants to provide team-building activities to promote collegiality.

COLLEGIALITY

Directing

Intervention Strategies

➤ **Directed Change**
Provide specific directive with the goal of changing the behavior and thus the results.
1. Identify the specific area(s) in which the teacher demonstrates a lack of collegiality.
2. Discuss with the teacher why he or she needs to work positively with the team.
3. Direct the teacher to work with the team on all future projects that require teamwork.
4. Follow up to ensure the teacher is working positively with the team.
5. Ask the teacher if he or she believes his or her actions are collegial.
6. Follow up to ensure the same behavior does not reoccur.

➤ **Provide Conflict Resolution**
Help the teacher resolve disputes through discussion and understanding and by jointly developing a resolution.
1. Encourage open dialogue in an attempt to reach an optimal solution.
2. Ask the teacher to explain to you his or her noncollegial responses to others.
3. Ask the teacher if there was a better way he or she could have handled the situation. If the teacher identifies new strategies, provide the support needed to implement them and if none are identified, provide alternatives you would like to see used.
4. Have the teacher articulate what he or she will do the next time to more cooperatively interact with others.
5. Monitor the teacher's interactions with others affirming the collegial responses or continuing to provide guidance if necessary.

COMPASSION

Encouraging

Intervention Strategies

> **Check for Understanding**
> *To avoid the inappropriate behavior, have the teacher paraphrase the instructions ensuring understanding of your expectations.*
> 1. Discuss with the teacher your perception of his or her lack of compassion in a specific situation.
> 2. Ask the teacher if he or she is aware of the impression others may have perceived based upon the actions or the conversation.
> 3. Discuss with the teacher alternative ways of responding that will be perceived as more empathetic.
> 4. Follow up frequently to ensure the teacher is attempting to implement the strategies discussed.
> 5. Continue to encourage the teacher to make the necessary changes.

> **Nonverbal Communication**
> *Use eye contact, body movement, or hand signals to gain the teacher's attention.*
> 1. Physically acknowledge lack of compassion via a facial expression such as a raised eyebrow or some other appropriate body language. If the problem persists, verbally confer with the teacher.
> 2. Make an effort to frequently be in areas where the teacher is interacting with others and then purposely acknowledge compassionate statements that demonstrate empathy by smiling, nodding, or gesturing a signal of satisfaction, like a thumbs-up.
> 3. Keep a written record of the positive interactions you can share with the teacher on a regular basis.

COMPASSION

Coaching

Intervention Strategies

> **Collaborate**
> *Have the teacher work together with others and self-assess how successful their solutions have been at resolving the problem.*
> 1. Discuss with the teacher the perceived lack of compassion.
> 2. Provide opportunities for others to serve as mentors to collaborate with the teacher in helping him or her develop alternative responses that would make empathy more apparent.
> 3. Continue to meet with the group helping the teacher to celebrate successes and provide modifications as necessary.

> **Reframing**
> *Help the teacher understand the impact of his or her words or actions and the need to consider alternatives.*
> 1. Help the teacher understand the perception of his or her lack of compassion.
> 2. Help the teacher reframe responses so the sense of empathy is apparent.
> 3. Role-play various scenarios with the teacher coaching him or her in the display of more appropriate responses.
> 4. Follow up frequently to see if improvements are occurring and provide assistance as needed.

COMPASSION

Structuring

Intervention Strategies

➤ **Ask Open-ended Questions**

Ask questions that provide for more than one simple answer, requiring the teacher to think more deeply about the behavior.

1. When trying to determine the reason behind the lack of compassion, ask questions such as "What were you thinking when you responded in what seemed to be an unempathetic way to _____?"
2. Ask "What affect do you think your response had on _____?"
3. Ask the teacher what he or she could have done differently.
4. Establish a verbal agreement with the teacher that he or she will begin taking ownership of responses that appear to lack empathy.
5. Monitor the teacher's attitude/behavior to determine if it improves or if greater intervention is necessary.

➤ **Reflective Journaling**

Provide a journal for the teacher to reflect on the behavior and determine a more positive course of action in the future.

1. Discuss with the teacher the perceived lack of compassion.
2. Ask the teacher to log his or her interactions and note where compassion was called for.
3. In those incidents where the teacher believes the response may have lacked compassion, have him or her reflect on ways the situation could have been handled better to demonstrate empathy.
4. Have the teacher leave a margin on the right-hand side of the journal page for you to respond to the journal entry.
5. If the reflection is rather shallow, elicit additional thoughts and feelings in a nondirective manner until the desired level of compassion is reached.
6. Conclude interactions with encouragement and affirmation.

COMPASSION

Directing

Intervention Strategies

➤ **Ask Convergent Questions**

Ask questions that allow for only very specific acceptable answers.

1. Without allowing for excuses, ask the teacher to explain why a perceived lack of compassion is an issue.
2. Continue asking "why" questions until you arrive at what seems to be the root cause.
3. Ask the teacher to clearly identify steps he or she will take to increase compassionate behavior.
4. Monitor the implementation steps.

➤ **Provide Conflict Resolution**

Help the teacher resolve disputes through discussion and understanding and by jointly developing a resolution.

1. In an attempt to uncover underlying feelings, ask the teacher to explain the response.
2. Bring the teacher and the offended party together to discuss the perceived lack of compassion.
3. Ask the offended party to express his or her feelings and ask the teacher to explain the initial response and the feelings behind what was said.
4. Ask both parties if there was something both could have changed to make the conversation more productive.
5. Have both parties articulate what they will do the next time to ensure that messages are understood and if there appears to be a lack of compassion, it is addressed.

CONTENT KNOWLEDGE

Encouraging

Intervention Strategies

➢ **Check for Understanding**
To avoid the inappropriate behavior, have the teacher paraphrase the instructions ensuring understanding of your expectations.
   1. Ask the teacher if he or she believes they have the appropriate content knowledge.
   2. Clarify the areas where the teacher has indicated his or level of knowledge of the content area is somewhat deficient.
   3. Provide support in the form of teacher assistance or training to overcome the deficiency.
   4. Check back with the teacher a week or so after the teacher has instituted the changes to determine if the intervention has been successful or if more support is needed.

➢ **Encourage Confidence**
Provide positive statements about the teacher's ability to achieve success using examples from previous experiences.
   1. Share with the teacher that you understand he or she is having difficulty teaching a specific element of the curriculum.
   2. Affirm that you are there to support the teacher.
   3. Ask what you might do to provide assistance.
   4. If the teacher is not clear on what needs to be done, collaboratively brainstorm to determine what might be helpful.
   5. Follow up quickly to ensure that whatever is needed has been provided and the teacher feels comfortable handling the lesson.

CONTENT KNOWLEDGE

Coaching

Intervention Strategies

➢ **Collaborate**
Have the teacher work together with others and self-assess how successful their solutions have been at solving the problem.
   1. With the help of the teacher, clearly identify the content area that needs the greatest support.
   2. As a team, generate a list of resources that could assist the teacher in the area of need.
   3. Categorize the list into resources in which the teacher feels comfortable and those he or she is not.
   4. Have the teacher select two to three resources that will assist in the area of need.
   5. After the teacher has made use of the resources, plan a classroom visit to check on their effectiveness.

➢ **Timely Identification of Inappropriate Behavior**
Address the concerning behavior as soon as is reasonably possible in order to stop it from reoccurring.
   1. Develop a paradigm of improvement rather than perfection.
   2. Schedule regular classroom visits for all teachers to help identify content area difficulty early.
   3. Review curriculum and pacing guides prior to classroom visits and then look for content in the lessons.
   4. Conduct 5–10 minute unannounced visits into the classroom and monitor the lesson content in an effort to identify concerns.
   5. Maintaining a supportive approach, correct minor concerns when you see them during these visits.
   6. When noted, be quick to acknowledge and affirm increased content knowledge.

CONTENT KNOWLEDGE

Structuring

Intervention Strategies

➢ **Individual Accountability**
Identify the area of concern and allow the teacher to personally address it.
1. Speak to the teacher privately to avoid drawing undue attention to his or her lack of content knowledge.
2. Ask the teacher in what content areas he or she needs the greatest support.
3. If necessary, provide possible suggestions for the teacher until an appropriate response is produced.
4. Praise the teacher's effort to increase his or her skill set and express your confidence in him or her as improvement is noted.

➢ **Suggest Activities**
Provide a list of activities the teacher could use as an alternative in the future.
1. Suggest that the teacher partner with a colleague who displays exemplary content knowledge, such as the department chair.
2. Divide the teachers into teams and have them collaboratively develop new methods for teaching difficult content and present them to one another at a faculty meeting or on an in-service day.
3. Provide opportunities for the teacher to observe others with demonstrated excellence in content knowledge at other schools and tie this into recertification points if possible.
4. Bring in outside consultants to provide in-services on effective methods to present difficult classroom content.

CONTENT KNOWLEDGE

Directing

Intervention Strategies

➢ **Ask "What" Questions**
Ask "what" questions until the teacher acknowledges the action and volunteers a solution.
1. Ask questions such as "In what areas of the content do you believe you need support?" or "In what specific areas do you see you need the most help?"
2. Follow up with additional questions such as "What level of support or training do you believe is needed?"
3. As assistance is provided, enthusiastically inquire of the teacher, "What are you learning and what are your plans to implement this in your classroom? What do you think will be the result?"
4. Monitor the teacher's implementation of what he or she has learned and determine if improvement is noted or if greater intervention is necessary.

➢ **Directed Change**
Provide specific directives with the goal of changing the behavior and thus the results.
1. Identify the specific area(s) the teacher demonstrates a lack of content knowledge.
2. Discuss with the teacher why he or she needs to have a thorough understanding of the content.
3. Provide resources to support the area(s) of concern, such as in-service training and workshops.
4. Follow up to ensure the teacher is using the provided resources.

CRITICAL THINKING SKILLS

Encouraging

Intervention Strategies

- ➢ **Assign a Mentor**
  Assign the teacher a mentor who demonstrates the desired behavior.
  1. Pair the teacher with a role model who excels in demonstrating effective critical thinking skills.
  2. Have the mentor and teacher collaboratively set goals for improving specific critical thinking skills.
  3. Check back frequently to monitor progress and make adjustments as needed.

- ➢ **Modeling**
  Demonstrate through example the behavior that is expected of the teacher.
  1. Frequently acknowledge and praise good critical thinking skills you have seen that teachers should emulate.
  2. Consider modeling a lesson to demonstrate specific critical thinking skills such as recognizing assumptions, evaluating arguments, and drawing conclusions.
  3. Be quick to praise the teacher when he or she demonstrates a deeper level of critical thinking.
  4. Be consistent in your praise as the teacher internalizes the desired critical thinking skills.

CRITICAL THINKING SKILLS

Coaching

Intervention Strategies

- ➢ **Brainstorm**
  Assist the teacher in thinking through alternative approaches to improve the behavior.
  1. Collaborate with the teacher to brainstorm realistic and specific alternatives that will enable him or her to think more critically when developing solutions to problems.
  2. Help the teacher determine the appropriate critical thinking skill needed.
  3. Encourage the teacher to try different strategies that model effective critical thinking.
  4. Have the teacher regularly touch base with you to discuss specific implementation of effective critical thinking skills, how they were demonstrated, and the results that followed.

- ➢ **Guided Problem-Solving**
  Provide opportunities to solve the problem by suggesting possible solutions and allowing the teacher to create alternatives.
  1. Identify the specific area in which the teacher has difficulty demonstrating effective critical thinking skills.
  2. Collaboratively identify the critical thinking skill deficits in specific terms and evaluate alternative strategies.
  3. Guide the teacher to think of ways to implement deeper levels of critical thinking.
  4. Provide encouragement to the teacher when you see evidence of increased levels of critical thinking.

CRITICAL THINKING SKILLS

Structuring

Intervention Strategies

➤ **Prioritize Concerns**
Provide a list of concerns in specific areas that need to be addressed by the teacher.
1. Meet with the teacher to identify and analyze the lack of critical thinking skills.
2. Identify specific areas in which critical thinking issues need to be addressed.
3. Prioritize the areas that need attention.
4. Collaboratively generate strategies that will assist the teacher in addressing these areas of need.
5. Check back frequently on the progress and make adjustments as needed.

➤ **Reflective Journaling**
Provide a journal for the teacher to reflect on the behavior and determine a more positive course of action in the future.
1. Discuss with the teacher the need for deeper critical thinking skills.
2. Ask the teacher to evaluate and keep a journal of how he or she used critical thinking skills throughout the day.
3. Encourage the teacher to determine whether he or she demonstrated appropriate critical thinking and, if not, what needs to be changed.
4. Explore alternative solutions.
5. Have the teacher journal what occurred, consider why it happened, explore possible meanings, and evaluate what could have been done differently.

CRITICAL THINKING SKILLS

Directing

Intervention Strategies

➤ **Ask "What" Questions**
Ask "what" questions until the teacher acknowledges the action and volunteers a solution.
1. Ask questions such as "What makes you think that?" or "What made you come to that conclusion?"
2. Listen carefully and do not formulate the next question until you have paid attention to the answer to the first.
3. Encourage specific and relevant responses with appropriate follow-up questions such as "What could you have done differently?"
4. Follow up with additional questions until you believe proper critical thinking by the teacher has been demonstrated.

➤ **Redirect**
Stop the teacher's inappropriate behavior and refocus the attention to the task at hand.
1. Call the teacher's attention to the lack of critical thinking in a specific situation.
2. Refocus the teacher's attention to a positive behavior that contributes to an appropriate solution to the problem where critical thinking skills were applied.
3. Clearly identify for the teacher what is expected.
4. Monitor the teacher's responses and praise as needed, elaborating on the positive elements of effective critical thinking.

CURRICULUM

Encouraging

Intervention Strategies

➢ **Assign a Mentor**
Assign the teacher a mentor who demonstrates the desired behavior.
1. Pair the teacher with a role model teaching the same subject and/or on the same grade level who excels in curriculum delivery.
2. With the mentor exhibiting respect and confidence in the teacher's abilities, have the pair schedule collaborative meetings to discuss curriculum goals and plans.
3. Check back frequently on the progress and make adjustments as needed.

➢ **Review Policies and Procedures**
Through verbal or written means, remind the teacher of specific written policies regarding the undesirable behavior.
1. Periodically remind everyone of the curriculum policies and procedures teachers are expected to follow.
2. Encourage the teacher to think beyond the immediate to see the long-term benefits of following the curriculum.
3. Make an effort to personally encourage teachers who may have been struggling with the curriculum when they have done a good job.

CURRICULUM

Coaching

Intervention Strategies

➢ **Assisted Goal Setting**
Help the teacher set achievable goals to improve behavior in a step-by-step manner.
1. Reinforce the need to adhere to the curriculum and identify where the noticeable behavior falls short.
2. Collaboratively brainstorm specific and realistic strategies in which the teacher can change his or her behavior.
3. Establish a time frame in which these strategies and goals can be implemented.
4. Provide feedback by periodically following up with the teacher to ensure compliance and establish new goals if necessary.

➢ **Guided Problem-Solving**
Provide opportunities to solve the problem by suggesting possible solutions and allowing the teacher to create alternatives.
1. Identify the specific problematic curriculum issue.
2. Collaborate with the teacher to define the problem in specific terms and evaluate alternative strategies.
3. Be clear on what the limits of the curriculum problem are so the discussion doesn't get bogged down by other issues.
4. Guide the teacher to see why it is critical to follow the prescribed curriculum.
5. Ask the teacher to brainstorm possible strategies that will enable him or her to follow the curriculum.
6. Provide encouragement to the teacher when you see evidence of successful strategy implementation.

CURRICULUM

Structuring

Intervention Strategies

➤ **Ask Self-evaluative Questions**
Ask questions that cause the teacher to self-reflect on the behavior.
1. Ask the teacher to provide a self-assessment of his or her efforts in following the curriculum.
2. Compare the teacher's self-evaluation with the expected standards for teaching the curriculum.
3. Point out the areas of compliance and noncompliance in order to bring appropriate alignment.
4. Monitor the progress on a regular basis and make necessary adjustments.

➤ **Provide a Timeline for Improvement**
Provide the teacher with a specific set of objectives for improvement that must be met along with clearly identifiable dates for attaining those objectives.
1. Highlight areas in which the teacher is appropriately and successfully implementing the curriculum.
2. Ask the teacher to assess whether the strategies he or she is using have been successful.
3. Guide the teacher to see how he or she can transfer those successful strategies over into the problematic curriculum area.
4. Agree upon specific target dates for transferring and implementing those strategies in the problem area.
5. After the teacher implements the strategies, periodically follow up to ensure compliance and establish new goals if necessary.

CURRICULUM

Directing

Intervention Strategies

➤ **Directed Change**
Provide specific directives with the goal of changing behavior and thus the results.
1. Identify the specific area in which the curriculum is being ignored.
2. Discuss with the teacher why the curriculum must be followed. (e.g., improves teaching and learning; required by school and/or district).
3. Discuss how the teacher can most effectively follow the curriculum.
4. Monitor and remind the teacher as necessary until he or she begins to practice the proper guidelines.

➤ **Outside Assistance**
Coordinate help from an outside source with the specific skills needed to help address the issue.
1. Keep an accurate record of the specific curriculum problem you have observed and identify which outside resource would best assist the teacher.
2. Meet with the teacher to discuss your curriculum concerns and let him or her know of your intention to provide outside assistance.
3. Meet with the outside resource to discuss your curriculum concerns and projected goals for the teacher and collectively determine the best strategy to approach the situation.
4. Permit the outside resource to work with the teacher.
5. Have the outside resource keep in touch with you to be sure that all are on the same page.
6. Follow up with the teacher to ensure that he or she is implementing the proper curriculum and offer further assistance if necessary.

DISINGENUOUSNESS

Encouraging

Intervention Strategies

➢ **Increase Physical Presence**
   Spend more time at the location where the problem behavior appears to occur most often.
   1. Arrange to be present in situations where the teacher's perceived disingenuousness is most noticeable.
   2. When you see the disingenuous attitude or behavior manifested, in a gentle way question the validity of the statement (e.g., "Are you sure about that?").
   3. If the disingenuousness seems to be ongoing, address the issue with the teacher.
   4. Continue to be present in the environment where the disingenuousness occurs most frequently.
   5. When the teacher is straightforward with communication, provide affirmation.

➢ **Provide Feedback**
   Give a timely assessment regarding what the teacher is doing correctly and what needs to be improved.
   1. Verbally give a specific description of how the teacher appears to be disingenuous.
   2. Ask the teacher if there are alternative ways to interact that would not be perceived as disingenuous.
   3. Guide the teacher to see where changes in behavior need to occur and provide specific alternatives as necessary.
   4. Collaboratively agree upon possible solutions to resolve the situation.
   5. Provide frequent encouragement and affirmation as progress is observed.

DISINGENUOUSNESS

Coaching

Intervention Strategies

➢ **Brainstorm**
   Assist the teacher in thinking through alternative approaches to improve the behavior.
   1. When the teacher engages in disingenuous behavior, help him or her brainstorm potential solutions to the problem.
   2. If the teacher is unable to identify solutions, brainstorm options and have him or her write them down as they are identified.
   3. Have the teacher choose one out of two to three options and identify which he or she will use when confronted with a similar situation in the future.
   4. Encourage follow-through and monitor the teacher's success.

➢ **Monitor Closely**
   Assess the teacher's progress as it relates to the given expectations.
   1. Determine the teacher's current perception of the situation.
   2. Ask the teacher to consider the situation from a different vantage point and if he or she is unable to do this, share an example.
   3. Encourage the teacher to verbalize some possible options for responding in a more truthful manner, particularly in stressful situations.
   4. Monitor the teacher closely to see if frequent praise of more genuine behavior elicits the desired change.

DISINGENUOUSNESS

Structuring

Intervention Strategies

➢ **Ask Open-ended Questions**
Ask questions that provide for more than one simple answer, requiring the teacher to think more deeply about the behavior.
1. Ask "what" questions until the teacher acknowledges his or her disingenuous behavior.
2. Ask a how question such as "How does your behavior benefit you or others?"
3. Ask "What would be a better way to be more truthful or sincere?"
4. Obtain a verbal agreement to stop the disingenuousness and be more forthright.
5. Monitor the teacher's attitude/behavior to determine if it improves or if greater intervention is necessary.

➢ **Individual Accountability**
Identify the area of concern and allow the teacher to personally address it.
1. Determine the teacher's motives behind the disingenuousness.
2. Ask yourself the following questions immediately after disingenuousness is discerned:
   • Do I feel annoyed? If so, attention getting may be the goal.
   • Do I feel intimidated? If so, power may be the goal.
   • Do I feel wronged or hurt? If so, revenge may be the goal.
   • Do I feel incapable of reaching the teacher? If so, helplessness may be the goal.
3. Respond appropriately:
   • If attention getting, ignore the behavior.
   • If power, do not allow open conflict.
   • If revenge, determine the reason.
   • If helplessness, provide opportunities for the teacher to succeed.

DISINGENUOUSNESS

Directing

Intervention Strategies

➢ **Confront**
Directly address the inappropriate behavior being very specific about what is expected and what is not appropriate.
1. Directly address the teacher's perceived disingenuous behavior.
2. Ask the teacher to explain the reasons for the disingenuousness.
3. Ask the teacher if there was a better way to handle the situation.
4. Have the teacher articulate what he or she will do next time to be more truthful or sincere.
5. Affirm the teacher's response if appropriate or provide alternatives if necessary.

➢ **Directed Change**
Provide specific directives with the goal of changing the behavior and thus the results.
1. Identify the specific area(s) the teacher needs to be more truthful.
2. Discuss why the teacher needs to be more transparent in his or her responses.
3. Assist the teacher in setting goals to be more genuine that meet your expectations.
4. Follow up to ensure the teacher is working to attain the goals.

DISLOYALTY

Encouraging

Intervention Strategies

➢ **Affirmative Statements**
Verbally acknowledge and emphasize the teacher's strengths and achievements.
1. In faculty meetings and other faculty communications, let teachers know how much you appreciate loyalty toward the school and others.
2. Praise the teacher when he or she demonstrates loyalty.
3. Emphasize that we are all in this together.
4. Find the positives and encourage the use of those strengths and abilities.

➢ **Provide Feedback**
Give a timely assessment regarding what the teacher is doing correctly and what needs to be improved.
1. Verbally give a specific description of how the teacher appears to be disloyal.
2. Ask the teacher if there are alternative ways to interact that would not be perceived as disloyal.
3. Guide the teacher to see where changes in behavior need to occur and provide specific alternatives as necessary.
4. Collaboratively agree upon possible solutions to resolve the situation.
5. Provide frequent encouragement and affirmation as progress is observed.

DISLOYALTY

Coaching

Intervention Strategies

➢ **Provide Leadership Opportunities**
Provide the teacher with opportunities to take on leadership roles related to the area of concern.
1. In areas of strength, assign the teacher to leadership positions on committees.
2. Coach the teacher in his or her leadership capacity and strategize with him or her about ways to keep meetings positive and aligned with the mission of the school.
3. Meet periodically to encourage the teacher's leadership skills and to particularly focus on statements or actions of loyalty.

➢ **Reframing**
Help the teacher understand the impact of his or her words or actions and the need to consider alternatives.
1. Help the teacher understand that disloyalty does not solve problems, but instead often exacerbates them while being destructive.
2. Help the teacher understand the impact of disloyal statements and how reframing can accomplish the same goal in a more productive way.
3. Work with the teacher to help him or her learn to reframe statements, removing judgment or condemnation. For example, help the teacher reframe a disloyal statement and rephrase it, eliminating divisiveness and instead producing cooperation.

DISLOYALTY

Structuring

Intervention Strategies

➤ **Negotiate**

Work to reach a compromise with the teacher through open discussion.

1. Discuss with the teacher the perceived lack of loyalty being demonstrated.
2. Listen to and address the teacher's concerns that have resulted in disloyal statements.
3. Accept the teacher at face value and don't try to negate his or her feelings.
4. While acknowledging feelings, help the teacher understand that his or her statements have been detrimental to others.
5. While respecting the teacher's right to his or her feelings, negotiate a means by which the teacher can make concerns known in an appropriate manner modifying public behavior that gives the impression of disloyalty.
6. Follow up frequently to see if the negotiated agreement is being adhered to and determine if modifications are required.

➤ **Prioritize Concerns**

Provide a list of concerns in specific areas that need to be addressed by the teacher.

1. Meet with the teacher to identify and analyze the appearance of disloyalty.
2. Identify specific areas in which the disloyalty has occurred and the impact of those statements or actions.
3. Collaboratively generate strategies that will assist the teacher in adopting a more loyal attitude.
4. Check back frequently on the progress and make adjustments as needed.

DISLOYALTY

Directing

Intervention Strategies

➤ **Manage Anger**

Require the teacher to participate in anger management strategies.

1. Have the teacher identify if there is any underlying anger that may be resulting in his or her disloyal statements.
2. Make clear to the teacher that the disloyal statements cannot be tolerated and we need to find more appropriate responses to deal with the apparent strong feelings that generate the disloyal attitude.
3. Brainstorm alternative strategies to deal with anger in a more appropriate manner and to demonstrate a greater degree of loyalty.
4. Help the teacher determine a safe place to "unload" when emotions intensify.

➤ **Redirect**

Stop the teacher's inappropriate behavior and refocus the attention to the task at hand.

1. Determine the cause of the disloyalty.
2. Call the teacher's attention to what he or she is doing that appears to be disloyal and how it is inappropriate.
3. Refocus the teacher's attention to positive behaviors that contribute to a greater degree of loyalty.
4. Clearly identify for the teacher what is expected.
5. Monitor the teacher and praise as needed, elaborating on the positive elements of the loyal attitude.

EMOTIONAL INAPPROPRIATENESS

Encouraging

Intervention Strategies

➤ **Humor**
Use humor to lighten a stressful situation.
1. Use humor when a teacher is continually overly emotional, overly serious, overly nervous, on the verge of misbehavior, or becoming frustrated.
2. Find ways to poke fun at yourself, allowing the teacher to understand your support although you do not approve of the behavior (e.g., "I can remember when someone told me 'Don't sweat the small stuff—it's all small stuff.' ").
3. Send a clear message that, although you are using humor to lighten the mood, you are confident the teacher *can* react in a more measured and controlled manner.

➤ **Provide Feedback**
Give a timely assessment regarding what the teacher is doing correctly and what needs to be improved.
1. Verbally give a specific description of how the teacher manifested an inappropriate emotional response in a particular situation and how it affected others.
2. Ask the teacher if there are alternative ways to interact that would not be perceived as overly emotional.
3. Guide the teacher to see where changes in behavior need to occur and provide specific alternatives as necessary.
4. Collaboratively agree upon possible solutions to resolve the situation.
5. Provide frequent encouragement and affirmation as progress is observed.

EMOTIONAL INAPPROPRIATENESS

Coaching

Intervention Strategies

➤ **Guided Problem-Solving**
Provide opportunities to solve the problem by suggesting possible solutions and allowing the teacher to create alternatives.
1. Identify and focus on the specific perceived inappropriate response so the discussion doesn't get bogged down by other issues.
2. Guide the teacher to see why it is critical to maintain self-control.
3. Ask the teacher to brainstorm possible strategies that will enable a more appropriate reaction in the future.
4. Provide encouragement when you see evidence of more appropriate emotional responses.

➤ **Reflect Verbal Responses**
Verbally reflect the essence of a teacher's argument in order to clarify his or her true feelings regarding the situation.
1. Ask the teacher, "What did you really mean when you said that?"
2. Listen carefully to the teacher's response and attempt to understand the underlying meaning.
3. Repeat the message back to the teacher and continue to seek clarity until true feelings are acknowledged.
4. Ask the teacher what steps can be taken to accept responsibility and avoid an inappropriate or overly emotional response.
5. Continue to reflect the teacher's responses until you can both agree on more appropriate ways for him or her to manage emotions.

EMOTIONAL INAPPROPRIATENESS

Structuring

Intervention Strategies

➤ **Ask Self-evaluative Questions**
Ask questions that cause the teacher to self-reflect on the behavior.
1. When you see a teacher reacting with inappropriate or overly emotional responses, inquire as to what is happening.
2. While providing support and empathy, try to determine the root cause of the reaction.
3. Model the attitude and behavior you would like to see displayed.
4. Look for opportunities to ask the teacher how he or she might feel if a similar situation happened to them.
5. Provide positive reinforcement when a positive response is elicited and gentle guidance of other alternatives if a negative response is received.

➤ **Reflective Journaling**
Provide a journal for the teacher to reflect on the behavior and determine a more positive course of action in the future.
1. Discuss with the teacher the perceived inappropriate emotional responses.
2. Ask the teacher to keep a journal and evaluate how he or she responded to others throughout the day.
3. In those incidents where the teacher believes the response may have been inappropriate, have him or her reflect on ways the situation could have been handled better.
4. Have the teacher leave a margin on the right hand side of the journal page for you to respond to the journal entry.
5. If the reflection is rather shallow, elicit additional thoughts and feelings in a nondirective manner until the desired level of understanding of appropriate emotional responses is reached. This could be done in writing through the journal or in person.
6. Conclude interactions with encouragement and affirmation.

EMOTIONAL INAPPROPRIATENESS

Directing

Intervention Strategies

➤ **Confront**
Directly address the inappropriate behavior being very specific about what is expected and what is not appropriate.
1. Encourage an open dialogue in an attempt to reach an optimal solution.
2. Ask the teacher to explain his or her inappropriate or overly emotional response.
3. Ask if there was a better way the teacher could have handled the situation.
4. Have the teacher articulate what he or she will do the next time to improve the reaction.
5. Affirm the teacher's response if appropriate or provide alternative actions if necessary.

➤ **Manage Anger**
Require the teacher to participate in anger management strategies.
1. Have the teacher identify what easily triggers his or her anger.
2. Brainstorm alternative strategies to deal with anger when it arises.
3. Help the teacher determine a safe place to "unload" when emotions intensify.
4. Refer the teacher to outside assistance if the problem persists.

EXAGGERATION

Encouraging

Intervention Strategies

➢ **Humor**

Use humor to lighten a stressful situation.
1. Establish rapport and relationship with the teacher through appropriate humor, being careful to never be cutting or sarcastic.
2. Find ways to poke fun at yourself to demonstrate when you have exaggerated your role in a situation and how it was not productive.
3. Send a clear message that, although you are using humor to lighten the mood, you are confident the teacher *can* be more grounded in reality, eliminating exaggeration.

➢ **Increase Physical Presence**

Spend more time at the location where the problem behavior appears to occur most often.
1. Arrange to be present in situations where the teacher's perceived exaggeration is most noticeable.
2. When you see the exaggeration being manifested, in a gentle way question the validity of the statement (i.e., "Are you sure about that?").
3. If the exaggeration seems to be ongoing, address the issue with the teacher.
4. Continue to be present in the environment where the exaggeration occurs most frequently.
5. When the teacher is straightforward with communication, provide affirmation.

EXAGGERATION

Coaching

Intervention Strategies

➢ **Reframing**

Help the teacher understand the impact of his or her words or actions and the need to consider alternatives.
1. Help the teacher understand the perception of his or her pattern of exaggeration.
2. Help the teacher reframe responses so they reflect reality.
3. Role-play various scenarios with the teacher coaching him or her in the display of more appropriate responses.
4. Follow up frequently to see if improvements are occurring and provide assistance as needed.

➢ **Self-Disclosure**

Allow the teacher an opportunity to personally identify the issue and determine alternatives to resolve the problem.
1. Meet with the teacher to discuss what appears to be a pattern of exaggeration.
2. Attempt to get the teacher to disclose the underlying reason why he or she tends to exaggerate.
3. Highlight times when you have heard the teacher not exaggerate but instead just present the facts and how the respondent was very receptive.
4. Be quick to encourage and affirm reality-based comments.
5. Follow up by asking the teacher to reveal how he or she felt after producing more reality-based statements.

EXAGGERATION

Structuring

Intervention Strategies

➤ **Prioritize Concerns**
Provide a list of concerns in specific areas that need to be addressed by the teacher.
1. Meet with the teacher to identify and analyze the pattern of exaggeration.
2. Identify specific areas in which exaggeration has occurred and the impact it has had on others.
3. Prioritize the areas that need attention.
4. Collaboratively generate strategies that will assist the teacher in adopting a more realistic attitude.
5. Check back frequently on the progress and make adjustments as needed.

➤ **Reflective Journaling**
Provide a journal for the teacher to reflect on the behavior and determine a more positive course of action in the future.
1. Discuss with the teacher the perceived exaggeration.
2. Ask the teacher to keep a journal and evaluate how he or she responded to others throughout the day.
3. In those incidents where the teacher believes the response may have been exaggerated, have him or her reflect on ways the situation could have been handled better.
4. Have the teacher leave a margin on the right hand side of the journal page for you to respond to the journal entry.
5. If the reflection is rather shallow, elicit additional thoughts and feelings in a nondirective manner until the desired level of reality is reached. This could be done in writing through the journal or in person.
6. Conclude interactions with encouragement and affirmation.

EXAGGERATION

Directing

Intervention Strategies

➤ **Confront**
Directly address the inappropriate behavior being very specific about what is expected and what is not appropriate.
1. Encourage an open exchange of information as it relates to the pattern of exaggeration in an attempt to curtail the problem.
2. Ask the teacher to explain his or her reasons for the exaggeration and if there was a better way to more accurately reflect what happened.
3. Have the teacher articulate what he or she will do the next time to diminish the behavior of exaggeration.
4. Affirm the teacher's response if appropriate or provide alternative actions if necessary.

➤ **Redirect**
Stop the teacher's inappropriate behavior and refocus the attention to the task at hand.
1. Call the teacher's attention to the pattern of exaggeration and how it is inappropriate.
2. Refocus the teacher's attention to more reality-based responses.
3. Clearly identify for the teacher what is expected.
4. Monitor the teacher and praise as needed, elaborating on the positive elements of reporting more realistic happenings.

FEEDBACK

Encouraging

Intervention Strategies

➤ **Affirmative Statements**
Verbally acknowledge and emphasize the teacher's strengths and achievements.
1. In faculty meetings and other faculty communications, continually praise and encourage appropriate parental feedback.
2. Praise the teacher when he or she attempts to use appropriate forms of feedback.
3. Remind the teacher of past accomplishments and successes that have resulted from positive feedback and encourage him or her to continue using these.

➤ **Provide Feedback**
Give a timely assessment regarding what the teacher is doing correctly and what needs to be improved.
1. Highlight areas in which the teacher has successfully used verbal/nonverbal feedback appropriately.
2. Ask the teacher to assess what he or she did to be successful before (i.e., why did they choose to use this method of feedback during a particular incident?).
3. Guide the teacher to see how he or she can transfer those methods of feedback to new situations.
4. After the teacher tries using the appropriate forms of feedback, periodically follow up with him or her to determine success levels and establish new goals if necessary.

FEEDBACK

Coaching

Intervention Strategies

➤ **Guided Empathy**
Help the teacher appreciate another's situation and to gain a better understanding of how he or she might feel in the same circumstance.
1. Begin by focusing on the way the teacher currently provides feedback.
2. Ask the teacher to explain the effectiveness of having a variety of strategies to provide feedback to students.
3. If the teacher responds negatively, guide the discussion to one about what a lack of effective feedback causes. Ask him or her to provide an example and tell how he or she felt when no feedback was received (e.g., when an administrator did not provide feedback on a classroom observation).
4. Help the teacher see how students make use of effective feedback and as such need a variety of effective feedback strategies.
5. Discuss possible varied strategies the teacher could use to be more effective in providing feedback to students.
6. Have the teacher incorporate the new strategies in the coming weeks and follow up by discussing the results.

➤ **Guided Problem-Solving**
Provide opportunities to solve the problem by suggesting possible solutions and allowing the teacher to create alternatives.
1. Identify the specific area in which the teacher has difficulty providing effective feedback.
2. Collaboratively identify the feedback deficits in specific terms and evaluate alternative strategies.
3. Guide the teacher to think of ways to implement alternative forms of feedback.
4. Provide encouragement to the teacher when you see evidence of increased or more appropriate feedback.

FEEDBACK

Structuring

Intervention Strategies

➤ **Prioritize Concerns**
Provide a list of concerns in specific areas that need to be addressed by the teacher.
1. Meet with the teacher to identify and analyze his or her feedback strategies.
2. Identify specific areas in which effective and timely feedback to students by the teacher is needed.
3. Prioritize which areas of teacher feedback need to be addressed first.
4. Collaboratively generate strategies that will assist the teacher in providing timely and effective feedback
5. Check back frequently on the progress and make adjustments as needed.

➤ **Reflective Journaling**
Provide a journal for the teacher to reflect on the behavior and determine a more positive course of action in the future.
1. Discuss with the teacher the perceived lack of feedback.
2. Ask the teacher to log feedback interactions with students and note his or her feelings about the process and the result.
3. Have the teacher leave a margin on the right hand side of the journal page for you to respond to the journal entry.
4. If the reflection is rather shallow, elicit additional thoughts and feelings in a nondirective manner until the desired level of understanding is reached. This could be done in writing through the journal or in person.
5. Conclude the interaction with encouragement and affirmation.

FEEDBACK

Directing

Intervention Strategies

➤ **Ask Closed Questions**
Ask questions that can normally be answered using a specific piece of information or a simple "yes" or "no."
1. Ask the teacher to respond to a direct question related to the manner in which he or she provides feedback.
2. Discuss the resultant feelings and behavior that emanate from appropriate and timely feedback.
3. Ask the teacher if the feedback he or she provides results in a desired response.
4. Follow up to ensure the teacher is using more appropriate feedback.

➤ **Redirect**
Stop the teacher's inappropriate behavior and refocus the attention to the task at hand.
1. Determine the cause of the poor verbal/nonverbal feedback.
2. Call the teacher's attention to what he or she is doing and that results in ineffective feedback.
3. Refocus the teacher's attention to positive behavior that contributes to appropriate verbal/nonverbal feedback.
4. Clearly identify for the teacher what is expected.
5. Monitor the teacher and praise as needed, elaborating on the positive elements of the verbal/nonverbal feedback.

GOAL SETTING

Encouraging

Intervention Strategies

➤ **Affirmative Statements**
  Verbally acknowledge and emphasize the teacher's strengths and achievements.
  1. Praise the teacher when he or she attempts to write professional goals.
  2. Emphasize the need for improvement in goal setting, not perfection.
  3. Capitalizing on the strengths of the teacher, find the positives and encourage the use of those abilities.

➤ **Encourage Confidence**
  Provide positive statements about the teacher's ability to achieve success using examples from previous experiences.
  1. Identify areas in which you have observed the teacher demonstrating confidence.
  2. Follow up with a discussion of your concerns regarding his or her perceived lack of goal setting.
  3. Relate the previously observed areas of strength to the current issue of the lack of goal setting, pointing out the confidence you have observed in other situations.
  4. Work with the teacher to apply the skills he or she has used in other areas to the area of goal setting.

GOAL SETTING

Coaching

Intervention Strategies

➤ **Assisted Goal Setting**
  Help the teacher set achievable goals to improve behavior in a step-by-step manner.
  1. Reinforce the need to develop goals.
  2. Collaboratively brainstorm specific and realistic goals that the teacher can slowly begin to implement.
  3. Establish benchmarks to monitor progress.
  4. Provide feedback by periodically following up with the teacher to ensure compliance and establish new goals if necessary.

➤ **Timely Identification of Inappropriate Behavior**
  Address the concerning behavior as soon as is reasonably possible in order to stop it from reoccurring.
  1. Schedule goal reviews for all teachers early in the year to help identify problem areas.
  2. Instruct teachers to review their goals each quarter to self-assess progress.
  3. Prior to going into the classroom for 5–10 minute unannounced visits, review the teacher's goals to see if progress is evident.
  4. Correct minor concerns when you see them during these visits, maintaining a supportive approach.
  5. When noted, be quick to acknowledge and affirm appropriate professional goal setting.

GOAL SETTING

Structuring

Intervention Strategies

➤ **Ask Self-evaluative Questions**
Ask questions that cause the teacher to self-reflect on the behavior.
1. Inquire if the teacher thinks his or her goal setting is sufficient.
2. When you see the teacher not developing appropriate professional goals, inquire as to what is happening, while trying to determine the root cause for the perceived lack of goal setting.
3. Ask the teacher to articulate the reasons why he or she is failing to set goals.
4. Compare the teacher's self-evaluation with your perceptions and together determine a plan for improvement.

➤ **Provide a Timeline for Improvement**
Provide the teacher with a specific set of objectives for improvement that must be met along with clearly identified dates for attaining those objectives.
1. Review the requirements for goal setting with the teacher.
2. Agree upon a time frame in which these goals will be implemented.
3. Provide feedback by periodically following up with the teacher to ensure compliance and establish new goals if necessary.

GOAL SETTING

Directing

Intervention Strategies

➤ **Directed Change**
Provide specific directives with the goal of changing the behavior and thus the results.
1. Identify the specific area(s) in which the teacher needs to improve related to goal setting.
2. Discuss why the teacher needs to set and monitor goals (e.g., improves teaching and student learning; it's required by school and/or district).
3. Assist the teacher in setting goals that meet your expectations.
4. Follow up to ensure the teacher is working to attain the goals.

➤ **Written Plan**
Develop a clear, concise plan for the teacher that contains specific goals and a timeline for achieving those goals.
1. Discuss with the teacher the need and requirements for setting instructional goals.
2. Establish a systematic plan for improving the teacher's goal setting.
3. Sign a written agreement containing a specific timeline for implementation of the teacher's goals.
4. Monitor the progress of the goal attainment and revise as needed.

GOSSIP

Encouraging

Intervention Strategies

➤ **Increase Physical Presence**
Spend more time at the location where the problem behavior appears to occur most often.
1. Arrange to be present in situations or locations where gossip typically occurs or where you anticipate its occurrence.
2. When you hear gossip, in a gentle way question the validity of the statement (e.g., "Are you sure about that?").
3. If the gossip seems to be ongoing, address the issue with the teacher.
4. Continue to be present in the environment where the gossip occurs most frequently.
5. When the teacher is straightforward with communication, provide affirmation.
6. In the strategies above, verbal communication is usually not needed; your physical proximity and presence is often enough to change the behavior.

➤ **Provide Feedback**
Give a timely assessment regarding what the teacher is doing correctly and what needs to be improved.
1. Verbally give a specific description of how the teacher's pattern of gossiping has affected others.
2. Ask the teacher if there is another alternative manner of interaction that would not be perceived as gossip.
3. Guide the teacher to see where changes in behavior need to occur and provide specific alternatives as necessary.
4. Collaboratively agree upon possible solutions to resolve the situation.
5. Provide frequent encouragement and affirmation as progress is observed.

GOSSIP

Coaching

Intervention Strategies

➤ **Appeal to Values**
Providing opportunity for self-reflection, discuss concerns and compare them to the positive values the teacher holds as demonstrated in the past.
1. Gently remind the teacher of what he or she holds dear in terms of value.
2. Inquire if the teacher thinks gossiping is appropriate.
3. Have the teacher think about situations where he or she has gossiped and identify more appropriate responses.
4. Praise positive responses, and if there is a lapse in appropriate behavior, compare the reaction to the teacher's more typical positive behavior.

➤ **Reframing**
Help the teacher understand the impact of his or her words or actions and the need to consider alternatives.
1. Help the teacher understand the perception of the ongoing gossiping.
2. Help the teacher reframe responses so that the conversation doesn't drift into gossip.
3. Role-play various scenarios with the teacher coaching him or her in the display of more appropriate responses.
4. Follow up frequently to see if improvements are occurring and provide assistance as needed.

GOSSIP

Structuring

Intervention Strategies

➢ **Prioritize Concerns**
Provide a list of concerns in specific areas that need to be addressed by the teacher.
1. Meet with the teacher to identify and analyze the incidents of perceived gossiping.
2. Identify specific areas or situations in which gossiping occurs.
3. Express clearly the need to not gossip and the affect it has on others and the organization.
4. Prioritize the areas that need attention.
5. Collaboratively generate strategies that will assist the teacher in avoiding gossip.
6. Check back frequently on the progress and make adjustments as needed.

➢ **Provide a Timeline for Improvement**
Provide the teacher with a specific set of objectives for improvement that must be met along with clearly identified dates for attaining those objectives.
1. Highlight statements that appear to be gossip.
2. Together with the teacher, develop alternative strategies to avoid gossiping.
3. Agree upon a timeline for improvement and follow up on a scheduled basis.

GOSSIP

Directing

Intervention Strategies

➢ **Confront**
Directly address the inappropriate behavior being very specific about what is expected and what is not appropriate.
1. Directly address the teacher's pattern of gossiping.
2. Ask the teacher to explain the reasons for the gossip.
3. Ask the teacher if there was a better way to handle the situation.
4. Have the teacher articulate what he or she will do next time to be able to avoid gossiping.
5. Affirm the teacher's response if appropriate or provide alternatives if necessary.

➢ **Redirect**
Stop the teacher's inappropriate behavior and refocus the attention to the task at hand.
1. Call the teacher's attention to the perceived gossip and how it is inappropriate.
2. Refocus the teacher's attention to positive behavior that avoids gossip.
3. Clearly identify for the teacher what is expected.
4. Monitor the teacher and praise as needed, elaborating on the positive elements of the new behavior.

IMPULSIVITY

Encouraging

Intervention Strategies

➤ **Increase Physical Presence**
Spend more time at the location where the problem behavior appears to occur most often.
1. Arrange to be present in situations where the teacher's impulsive behavior typically occurs or where you anticipate its occurrence.
2. Position yourself near the locations at critical times where the teacher is assigned but may not be fulfilling duties.
3. Frequently visit the classroom of the teacher who may be impulsive.
4. In the strategies above, verbal communication is usually not needed; your physical proximity and presence is often enough to change the behavior.

➤ **Review Policies and Procedures**
Through verbal or written means, remind the teacher of specific written policies regarding the undesirable behavior.
1. Periodically remind everyone of the principles of self-control teachers are expected to follow.
2. Encourage the teacher to think beyond the immediate to see the long-term benefits of maintaining self-control.
3. Make an effort to personally encourage teachers who may have been struggling with impulsivity when they have done a good job.

IMPULSIVITY

Coaching

Intervention Strategies

➤ **Appeal to Values**
Providing opportunity for self-reflection, discuss concerns and compare them to the positive values the teacher holds as demonstrated in the past.
1. Gently remind the teacher of what he or she holds dear in terms of value.
2. Inquire if the teacher thinks impulsive responses are appropriate.
3. Have the teacher think about his or her impulsive behavior and identify more appropriate responses.
4. Praise positive responses, and if there is a lapse in appropriate behavior, compare the reaction to the teacher's more typical restrained conduct.

➤ **Timely Identification of Inappropriate Behavior**
Address the concerning behavior as soon as is reasonably possible in order to stop it from reoccurring.
1. When you see the teacher display an impulsive behavior, privately bring it to his or her attention as soon as possible.
2. Remind the teacher of possible alternative behaviors that have been previously discussed.
3. Be quick to acknowledge and affirm nonimpulsive or appropriate measured responses.

IMPULSIVITY

Structuring

Intervention Strategies

➢ **Individual Accountability**

Identify the area of concern and allow the teacher to personally address it.

1. Speak to the teacher privately to avoid drawing undue attention to his or her impulsivity and to let him or her know what you observed.
2. Ask the teacher what would help him or her be less impulsive.
3. If necessary, provide possible suggestions for the teacher until an appropriate response is produced.
4. Affirm the teacher's effort to think through situations and express your confidence as improvement is noted.

➢ **Provide Alternatives**

Provide viable, appropriate options to the current inappropriate behaviors of the teacher.

1. Collaboratively brainstorm realistic and specific alternatives to potential impulsive decisions before they arise.
2. Help the teacher determine which alternative might be more appropriate and when.
3. Encourage the teacher to try different alternatives.
4. Have the teacher regularly touch base with you to discuss specific situations, how they were handled, and the results that followed.

IMPULSIVITY

Directing

Intervention Strategies

➢ **Confront**

Directly address the inappropriate behavior being very specific about what is expected and what is not appropriate.

1. Encourage open dialogue in an attempt to reach an optimal solution.
2. Ask the teacher to explain the impulsive response.
3. Ask the teacher if there was a better way the situation could have been handled.
4. Have the teacher articulate what he or she will do the next time to avoid impulsiveness.
5. Affirm the teacher's response if appropriate or provide alternative actions if necessary.

➢ **Directed Change**

Provide specific directives with the goal of changing the behavior and thus the results.

1. Identify the specific area in which the teacher is being impulsive.
2. Discuss with the teacher why impulsiveness may not always be in the best interest of the students.
3. Discuss strategies that will enable the teacher to think before he or she acts.
4. Remind the teacher as necessary until he or she begins to practice proper self-control.

INDIFFERENCE

Encouraging

Intervention Strategies

➢ **Modeling**
  Demonstrate through example the behavior that is expected of the teacher.
  1. Model commitment to the staff and to the organization.
  2. Frequently acknowledge and praise commitment you have seen that teachers should emulate.
  3. Be quick to praise the teacher when he or she demonstrates commitment and/or enthusiasm.
  4. Be consistent in your praise as the teacher internalizes the desired attitude.

➢ **Provide Feedback**
  Give a timely assessment regarding what the teacher is doing correctly and what needs to be improved.
  1. Highlight areas in which the teacher has previously been excited.
  2. Ask the teacher to assess to what that excitement can be attributed.
  3. Guide the teacher to determine how he or she can transfer that excitement into the current situation.
  4. Provide frequent encouragement and affirmation as progress is observed.

INDIFFERENCE

Coaching

Intervention Strategies

➢ **Appeal to Values**
  Providing opportunities for self-reflection, discuss concerns and compare them to the positive values the teacher holds as demonstrated in the past.
  1. Gently remind the teacher of what he or she holds dear in terms of value.
  2. Inquire if the teacher thinks indifference is an appropriate response.
  3. Have the teacher think about his or her indifference and identify ways to become more committed again.
  4. Praise engagement and if there is a lapse of commitment, compare the reaction to the teacher's more typical committed behavior.

➢ **Guided Problem-Solving**
  Provide opportunities to solve the problem by suggesting possible solutions and allowing the teacher to create alternatives.
  1. Identify the specific indifferent attitude.
  2. Collaborate with the teacher to define the indifference in specific terms and evaluate alternative strategies.
  3. Guide the teacher to see why it is critical to demonstrate commitment.
  4. Ask the teacher to brainstorm possible strategies that will reignite his or her excitement.
  5. Provide encouragement to the teacher when you see evidence of successful strategy implementation.

INDIFFERENCE

Structuring

Intervention Strategies

➤ **Ask Self-evaluative Questions**
Ask questions that cause the teacher to self-reflect on the behavior.
1. Ask self-evaluative questions that help the teacher recognize the indifference demonstrated in his or her attitude.
2. Assist the teacher in determining some ways to rejuvenate the excitement he or she once had.
3. Encourage the teacher to implement one or more solutions to resolve the perceived lack of commitment.
4. Provide positive reinforcement when a positive response is elicited and gentle guidance of other alternatives if a negative response is received.

➤ **Individual Accountability**
Identify the area of concern and allow the teacher to personally address it.
1. Speak to the teacher privately to avoid drawing undue attention to his or her lack of commitment.
2. Ask the teacher what could be done to increase commitment.
3. If necessary, provide possible suggestions for the teacher until an appropriate response is produced.
4. Affirm the teacher's effort to demonstrate commitment and express your confidence as improvement is noted.

INDIFFERENCE

Directing

Intervention Strategies

➤ **Ask Closed Questions**
Ask questions that can normally be answered using a very specific piece of information or a simple "yes" or "no."
1. Ask the teacher questions such as "Are you committed to this activity we're involved in? Can you understand why I don't perceive that you are committed?"
2. Ask the teacher if the perceived indifferent behavior is in the best interest of others or the school and explain why it cannot be tolerated.
3. Express your expectations of the need for commitment to the school, its students, and the staff.
4. Follow up to ensure compliance as needed.

➤ **Written Plan**
Develop a clear, concise plan for the teacher that contains specific goals and a timeline for achieving those goals.
1. Discuss with the teacher what is expected in terms of commitment.
2. Establish a systematic plan for the seeming indifference.
3. Sign a written agreement with the teacher that contains a specific timeline for implementation.
4. Monitor and revise the plan as necessary.

INFLEXIBILITY

Encouraging

Intervention Strategies

➤ **Humor**
   Use humor to lighten a stressful situation.
   1. Use humor when the teacher is continually inflexible, is overly nervous about adapting to change, is on the verge of giving up on trying to change, or is becoming frustrated with his or her skillset.
   2. Find ways to poke fun at yourself, allowing the teacher to understand you empathize but want him or her to be adaptable (e.g., tell a humorous story—"I can remember when I was a teacher and I tried using _____ for the first time.").
   3. Send a clear message that, although you are using humor to lighten the mood, you are confident the teacher *can* be more flexible.

➤ **Provide Feedback**
   Give a timely assessment regarding what the teacher is doing correctly and what needs to be improved.
   1. Highlight areas in which the teacher has successfully adapted to changing situations.
   2. Ask the teacher to assess what he or she did to be successful during those times of change.
   3. Guide the teacher to see how he or she can transfer those successful strategies into new situations.
   4. After the teacher tries new strategies demonstrating flexibility, periodically follow up to provide encouragement and affirmation.

INFLEXIBILITY

Coaching

Intervention Strategies

➤ **Monitor Closely**
   Assess the teacher's progress as it relates to the given expectations.
   1. Determine the teacher's current perception of the situation.
   2. Ask the teacher to consider the situation from a different vantage point and if he or she is unable to do this, share an example.
   3. Encourage the teacher to verbalize some possible options on how he or she could be more flexible.
   4. Monitor the teacher closely to see if frequent praise of increased flexibility elicits the desired change.

➤ **Reflect Verbal Responses**
   Verbally reflect the essence of a teacher's argument in order to clarify his or her true feelings regarding the situation.
   1. In order to get the teacher to clarify underlying meaning, ask him or her, "If I hear you correctly, you are saying _____."
   2. Listen carefully to the teacher's response and attempt to understand the underlying meaning.
   3. Repeat the message back to the teacher and continue to seek clarity until true feelings are acknowledged.
   4. Ask the teacher what steps can be taken to ensure the inflexible behavior does not continue to occur.
   5. Continue to reflect the teacher's responses until you can both agree on more appropriate ways to demonstrate flexibility.

INFLEXIBILITY

Structuring

Intervention Strategies

➤ **Individual Accountability**
Identify the area of concern and allow the teacher to personally address it.
1. Speak to the teacher privately to avoid drawing undue attention to his or her lack of flexibility.
2. Ask the teacher what he or she could do differently to adapt to the situation.
3. If necessary, provide possible suggestions for the teacher until an appropriate response is produced.
4. Praise the teacher's effort to be flexible and express your confidence in him or her as improvement is noted.

➤ **Persuade**
Use reasoning to help the teacher understand the need for change.
1. Affirm your esteem for the teacher as part of the school and point out positive contributions.
2. State your specific concerns about the teacher's inflexible behavior or attitude.
3. Ensure that the teacher understands the need to make changes.
4. Offer possible alternatives to the current behavior or attitude that would result in better relationships.
5. Continue the discussion until you have persuaded the teacher that a more flexible attitude is necessary.
6. Follow up with the teacher to ensure more flexibility is demonstrated.

INFLEXIBILITY

Directing

Intervention Strategies

➤ **Ask Convergent Questions**
Ask questions that allow for only very specific acceptable answers.
1. Without allowing for excuses, ask the teacher to specifically explain why being flexible is an issue.
2. Continue asking "why" questions until you arrive at what seems to be the root cause of the issue.
3. Ask the teacher to clearly identify steps that will increase his or her flexibility.
4. Monitor the implementation steps.

➤ **Directed Change**
Provide specific directives with the goal of changing the behavior and thus the results.
1. Identify the specific area(s) in which the teacher demonstrates inflexibility.
2. Discuss why the teacher needs to be more flexible.
3. Identify specific steps the teacher needs to use to be more flexible.
4. Monitor the teacher frequently to ensure satisfactory progress in terms of flexibility.

INITIATIVE

Encouraging

Intervention Strategies

➢ **Affirmative Statements**
Verbally acknowledge and emphasize the teacher's strengths and achievements.
1. In faculty meetings and other faculty communications, let teachers know how much you appreciate initiative in activities that bring a positive light to the school.
2. Point out how helpful the teacher's contributions have been in the past.
3. Praise the teacher when you observe him or her attempting to initiate a contribution.

➢ **Provide Feedback**
Give a timely assessment regarding what the teacher is doing correctly and what needs to be improved.
1. Highlight areas in which the teacher has previously demonstrated initiative.
2. Ask the teacher to assess those areas in which he or she has previously shown initiative and discuss the results.
3. Guide the teacher to see how he or she can transfer those successful strategies into the new situation.
4. After the teacher implements the new approach, periodically follow up providing encouragement and affirmation.

INITIATIVE

Coaching

Intervention Strategies

➢ **Provide Leadership Opportunities**
Provide the teacher with opportunities to take on leadership roles related to the area of concern.
1. Meet with the teacher to discuss opportunities to contribute in a leadership capacity.
2. Discuss with the teacher exactly what you expect to see in terms of new plans and activities in the agreed-upon assignment.
3. Provide support and meet regularly with the teacher about the group he or she is leading and address any issues that arise, particularly in regard to initiative or the lack thereof.

➢ **Self-Disclosure**
Allow the teacher an opportunity to personally identify the issue and determine alternatives to resolve the problem.
1. Meet with the teacher to discuss what appears to be a lack of initiative.
2. Attempt to get the teacher to disclose the underlying reason why he or she may not be contributing.
3. Encourage risk taking in team and group meetings where the teacher has an idea that would be valuable.
4. Highlight times when you have observed initiative and the resultant positive outcome.
5. Be quick to encourage and affirm appropriate risk taking.
6. Follow up by asking the teacher to reveal how he or she felt after taking a risk and demonstrating more initiative.

INITIATIVE

Structuring

Intervention Strategies

➤ **Individual Accountability**
Identify the area of concern and allow the teacher to personally address it.
1. Speak to the teacher privately to avoid drawing undue attention to his or her lack of initiative.
2. Ask the teacher what he or she could do differently.
3. If necessary, provide possible suggestions for the teacher until an appropriate response is produced.
4. Praise the teacher's effort to initiate and contribute to the greater cause and express your confidence in him or her as improvement is noted.

➤ **Suggest Activities**
Provide a list of activities the teacher could use as an alternative in the future.
1. Suggest that the teacher partner with a colleague who displays exemplary initiative.
2. Suggest situations where the teacher can show initiative.
3. Provide an environment where it is safe to take risks in sharing new ideas.

INITIATIVE

Directing

Intervention Strategies

➤ **Confront**
Directly address the inappropriate behavior being very specific about what is expected and what is not appropriate.
1. Ask the teacher to explain his or her lack of initiative.
2. Ask the teacher if there are ways he or she can contribute.
3. Have the teacher articulate what he or she will do the next time there are opportunities to take initiative.
4. Affirm the teacher's response if appropriate or provide alternative actions if necessary.

➤ **Outside Assistance**
Coordinate help from an outside source with the specific skills needed to address the issue.
1. Keep an accurate report of the lack of contribution you have observed and identify which outside resource would best assist the teacher.
2. Meet with the teacher to discuss your concerns and let him or her know your intention to provide assistance.
3. Bring in outside assistance, discuss your concerns and projected goals, collectively determine the best strategy to approach the situation, and permit that person to work with the teacher.
4. Have the outside resource keep in touch with you to be sure that all are on the same page.
5. Follow up with the teacher to ensure that he or she is implementing the plan and offer further assistance if necessary.

INSENSITIVITY

Encouraging

Intervention Strategies

➤ **Affirmative Statements**
Verbally acknowledge and emphasize the teacher's strengths and achievements.
1. Praise the teacher when appropriate sensitivity is displayed.
2. Remind the teacher of his or her past sensitivity to others and try to instill the idea that having been sensitive in one situation, he or she can express that same attitude in others.
3. Encourage the teacher to continue to exhibit sensitivity to others.

➤ **Modeling**
Demonstrate through example the behavior that is expected of the teacher.
1. In conversations with the teacher, model a sensitive understanding as it relates to others and their behaviors and/or needs.
2. Be quick to praise the teacher when he or she demonstrates appropriate responses to others.
3. Be consistent in your praise until the teacher internalizes more sensitive responses.

INSENSITIVITY

Coaching

Intervention Strategies

➤ **Brainstorm**
Assist the teacher in thinking through alternative approaches to improve the behavior.
1. Collaboratively brainstorm more sensitive responses to situations that might arise.
2. Help the teacher determine which alternative might be more appropriate and when.
3. Encourage the teacher to try different alternatives.
4. Have the teacher regularly touch base with you to discuss specific situations, how they were handled, and the results that followed.

➤ **Guided Empathy**
Help the teacher appreciate another's situation and to gain a better understanding of how he or she might feel in the same circumstance.
1. As your relationship develops with the teacher, ask questions to discern his or her level of identification, understanding, and empathy toward others.
2. In areas that seem undefined, explain how you might respond demonstrating sensitivity and kindness.
3. Ask the teacher how he or she would feel if the shoe were on his or her foot, if he or she was going through the same thing.
4. After encountering various situations, have the teacher share with you what he or she is encountering with various colleagues or students and how he or she can better respond to them in their circumstances.

INSENSITIVITY

Structuring

Intervention Strategies

➢ **Ask Self-evaluative Questions**
   Ask questions that cause the teacher to self-reflect on the behavior.
   1. At a regularly scheduled faculty meeting, distribute to everyone a self-assessment that includes questions directly dealing with the ability to empathize with others.
   2. When you see a teacher not empathizing with another, "befriend" him or her and model the attitude and behavior that you would like to see displayed.
   3. Look for opportunities to ask the teacher how he or she might feel if such and such happened to them. Provide positive reinforcement when a positive response is elicited and gentle guidance of other alternatives if a negative response is received.

➢ **Reflective Journaling**
   Provide a journal for the teacher to reflect on the behavior and determine a more positive course of action in the future.
   1. Discuss with the teacher the perceived insincerity.
   2. Ask the teacher to keep a journal and evaluate how he or she responded to others throughout the day.
   3. Encourage the teacher to determine whether he or she demonstrated the ability to empathize with others or if not, what does he or she think needs to be changed.
   4. Explore alternative solutions.
   5. Have the teacher journal incidents that occurred, consider why they happened, explore possible meanings, and evaluate what could have been done differently.
   6. Follow up on a regular basis to ensure continued growth.

INSENSITIVITY

Directing

Intervention Strategies

➢ **Ask Convergent Questions**
   Ask questions that allow for only very specific acceptable answers.
   1. Ask the teacher if he or she believes sensitivity was demonstrated in a specific situation.
   2. Without allowing for excuses, ask for an explanation of why the teacher has difficulty being sensitive to others.
   3. Continue asking questions until you arrive at what seems to be the root cause for the insensitivity.
   4. Ask the teacher to clearly identify steps he or she will take to increase sensitivity.
   5. Monitor the implementation steps.

➢ **Confront**
   Directly address the inappropriate behavior being very specific about what is expected and what is not appropriate.
   1. Ask questions such as "What happened?", "How did you react and what was the response of the other person?", "How do you think you'd feel if they did that to you?", How do you think they feel now?"
   2. Listen carefully and do not formulate the next question until you have paid attention to the response to the first.
   3. Encourage specific and relevant responses with appropriate follow-up questions such as "What could you have done differently?"
   4. Provide additional support and assistance to ensure the teacher is aware of others' feelings followed by the adoption of a more sensitive attitude.

INSINCERITY

Encouraging

Intervention Strategies

➢ **Modeling**
   Demonstrate through example the behavior that is expected of the teacher.
   1. During faculty meetings or other faculty communications, frequently acknowledge and praise sincere behaviors you have seen in others.
   2. Verbally acknowledge and praise sincerity in others so the teacher can be reminded of what is expected.
   3. Be quick to praise the teacher when he or she demonstrates sincere behavior.
   4. Be consistent in your praise as the teacher internalizes the desired qualities and begins to respond in a more sincere manner.

➢ **Provide Feedback**
   Give a timely assessment regarding what the teacher is doing correctly and what needs to be improved.
   1. Verbally give a specific description of how the teacher was insincere in a specific situation.
   2. Inform the teacher how the insincere behavior affected others.
   3. Ask the teacher if there are alternative ways to interact that would not be perceived as insincere.
   4. Guide the teacher to see where changes in behavior need to occur and provide specific alternatives as necessary.
   5. Collaboratively agree upon possible solutions to resolve the situation.
   6. Provide frequent encouragement and affirmation as progress is observed.

INSINCERITY

Coaching

Intervention Strategies

➢ **Appeal to Values**
   Provide opportunity for self-reflection, discuss concerns, and compare them to the positive values the teacher holds as demonstrated in the past.
   1. Gently remind the teacher of what he or she holds dear in terms of value.
   2. Inquire if the teacher thinks insincerity is appropriate.
   3. Have the teacher think about his or her insincere response and identify a more appropriate attitude.
   4. Praise positive responses, and if there is a lapse in appropriate behavior, compare the reaction to the teacher's more typical sincere behavior.

➢ **Guided Problem-Solving**
   Provide opportunities to solve the problem by suggesting possible solutions and allowing the teacher to create alternatives.
   1. Identify the specific insincere attitude that is interfering with healthy interpersonal relationships.
   2. Collaborate with the teacher to define the insincerity in specific terms and evaluate alternative strategies.
   3. Guide the teacher to determine possible strategies that will enable him or her to reflect a more sincere attitude.
   4. Provide encouragement to the teacher when you see evidence of more sincere behavior.

INSINCERITY

Structuring

Intervention Strategies

➤ **Ask Open-ended Questions**

Ask questions that provide for more than one simple answer, requiring the teacher to think more deeply about the behavior.

1. When trying to determine the reason behind the frequent insincerity, ask questions such as "Do you think there was anything in your conversation with 'x' that might be interpreted as insincere? What do you think it was?"
2. Follow up by asking "Is there anything you think you could do differently in the future?"
3. Monitor the teacher's attitude/behavior to determine if it improves or if greater intervention is necessary.

➤ **Persuade**

Use reasoning to help the teacher understand the need for change.

1. Affirm your esteem for the teacher as part of the school and point out some positive contributions.
2. State your specific concerns about the teacher's insincere behavior or attitude.
3. Explain that if the teacher had handled the situation with a little more sincerity how it would have contributed to improved relationships.
4. Ask for the teacher's opinion on the reasons for the attitude.
5. Continue the discussion until you have persuaded the teacher on at least one area where the attitude or behavior can improve.
6. Follow up with the teacher to ensure that the attitude is improving.

INSINCERITY

Directing

Intervention Strategies

➤ **Ask Closed Questions**

Ask questions that can normally be answered using a specific piece of information or a simple "yes" or "no."

1. Ask the teacher questions such as "Were you as open and forthcoming as you could have been in 'x' situation?"
2. Ask the teacher if the perceived insincere behavior is in the best interest of others or the school and explain why it cannot be tolerated in a positive working environment.
3. Express your expectations of the need for sincerity in relationships with the students and staff.
4. Follow up to ensure compliance as needed.

➤ **Outside Assistance**

Coordinate help from an outside source with the specific skills needed to help address the issue.

1. Keep a record of the specific problems of insincerity you have observed and identify outside resources to best assist the teacher.
2. Meet with the teacher to discuss your concerns and let him or her know of your intention to provide assistance.
3. After discussing your concerns and projected goals with the outside resource, collectively determine the best strategy to approach the situation and then permit that person to work with the teacher.
4. Have the outside resource keep in touch with you to be sure that all are on the same page.
5. Follow up and encourage the teacher as you see more sincere behavior demonstrated.

INSTRUCTIONAL STRATEGIES

Encouraging

Intervention Strategies

➤ **Modeling**
Demonstrate through example the behavior that is expected of the teacher.
1. During faculty meetings or in other faculty communications, frequently acknowledge and praise good instructional practices that teachers should emulate.
2. While conducting classroom visits, verbally acknowledge and praise the use of differentiation in others' classrooms so the teacher can be reminded of what is expected.
3. Consider modeling a lesson to demonstrate instructional strategies the teacher is not currently using.

➤ **Provide Feedback**
Give a timely assessment regarding what the teacher is doing correctly and what needs to be improved.
1. Highlight areas in which the teacher has successfully used a new instructional strategy.
2. Ask the teacher to assess whether the instructional strategies he or she is already using have been successful.
3. Guide the teacher to see how he or she can transfer those earlier implementation skills in the employment of new instructional strategies.
4. After the teacher implements a new instructional strategy, periodically follow up offering encouragement, affirmation, and assistance if necessary.

INSTRUCTIONAL STRATEGIES

Coaching

Intervention Strategies

➤ **Assisted Goal Setting**
Help the teacher set achievable goals to improve behavior in a step-by-step manner.
1. Reinforce the need to use a variety of instructional strategies to meet the diverse needs of the students.
2. Collaboratively identify specific and realistic instructional strategies the teacher can slowly begin to implement into his or her classes.
3. Establish benchmarks to monitor progress.
4. Provide feedback by periodically following up with the teacher to ensure the implementation of varied instructional strategies and establish new goals if necessary.

➤ **Reflect Verbal Responses**
Verbally reflect the essence of the teacher's argument in order to clarify his or her true feelings regarding the situation.
1. Ask the teacher to explain the instructional issue as he or she sees it.
2. Reflect to the teacher by restating the key issues you heard in the explanation.
3. Ask the teacher if you correctly summarized what the issue seems to be.
4. Respond to the teacher with a list of potential instructional strategies to improve student learning.
5. Allow the teacher to choose from the list and apply at least one new instructional strategy.
6. Have the teacher report back to you on the level of success of the new instructional strategy.
7. Provide other alternatives as needed.

INSTRUCTIONAL STRATEGIES

Structuring

Intervention Strategies

➤ **Orchestrate Positive Peer Reinforcement**

Enlist fellow teachers to provide encouragement and affirmation for the teacher having difficulty.

1. Pair the teacher with a role model teaching the same subject and/or on the same grade level that excels in using a variety of instructional strategies.
2. Provide time during the instructional day for the two to collaborate.
3. Have the mentor and the teacher collaboratively set goals for trying different instructional strategies in the class.
4. Check back frequently on the progress and make adjustments as needed.

➤ **Provide Alternatives**

Provide viable, appropriate options to the current inappropriate behaviors of the teacher.

1. Collaboratively brainstorm additional instructional strategies the teacher can add to his or her arsenal to most effectively meet the needs of all students.
2. Help the teacher determine which alternative might be more appropriate and when.
3. Encourage the teacher to try the different alternatives in upcoming lessons.
4. Have the teacher regularly touch base with you to discuss the instructional strategies used, how successful they were, and the results that followed.

INSTRUCTIONAL STRATEGIES

Directing

Intervention Strategies

➤ **Confront**

Directly address the inappropriate behavior being very specific about what is expected and what is not appropriate.

1. Ask the teacher to explain the reason for only using a limited number of instructional strategies.
2. Ask the teacher if there are other strategies he or she would like to try. If the teacher identifies new strategies, provide the support needed to implement them and if none are identified, provide alternatives you would like to see used.
3. Have the teacher articulate what he or she will do in the future to use a wider variety of instructional strategies.
4. Monitor lesson plans and visit the classroom to insure implementation.

➤ **Outside Assistance**

Coordinate help from an outside source with the specific skills needed to address the issue.

1. Keep an accurate record of the specific problems you have observed related to the use of limited instructional strategies and identify which outside resource would best assist the teacher.
2. Meet with the teacher to discuss your instructional strategy concerns and let him or her know of your intention to provide assistance.
3. Discuss your concerns and projected goals for the teacher, collectively determine the best strategy to approach the situation, and then permit the outside resource to work with the teacher.
4. Have the outside resource keep in touch with you to be sure that all are on the same page.
5. Follow up with the teacher to ensure he or she is implementing a variety of effective instructional strategies.

JUDGMENTAL

Encouraging

Intervention Strategies

➢ **Humor**
Use humor to lighten a stressful situation.
1. Establish a rapport and relationship with the teacher through appropriate humor, being careful to never be cutting or sarcastic.
2. Find ways to poke fun at yourself to demonstrate similar times when you've been judgmental in the past and how it was not productive.
3. Send a clear message that, although you are using humor to lighten the mood, you are confident the teacher *can* demonstrate a nonjudgmental attitude.

➢ **Nonverbal Communication**
Use eye contact, body movement, or hand signals to gain the teacher's attention.
1. Physically acknowledge the judgmental attitude via raised eyebrows, a scowl, a shake of the head, or other appropriate body language.
2. Make an effort to frequently be in areas where the teacher is interacting with others and then purposely acknowledge a more accepting or nonjudgmental attitude by smiling, nodding, or gesturing a signal of satisfaction, like a thumbs-up.
3. Keep a written record of the positive interactions you can share with the teacher on a regular basis.

JUDGMENTAL

Coaching

Intervention Strategies

➢ **Guided Empathy**
Help the teacher appreciate another's situation and to gain a better understanding of how he or she might feel in the same circumstance.
1. As your relationship develops with the teacher, ask questions to discern the level of identification and understanding of his or her judgmental manner toward others.
2. Explain how you might express your opinions with more sensitivity and kindness rather than being judgmental.
3. Ask the teacher how he or she would feel if the shoe were on his or her foot, if he or she was going through the same thing.
4. After encountering various situations, have the teacher share with you what he or she is encountering with various colleagues or students and how he or she can better respond to them in their circumstances.

➢ **Guided Problem-Solving**
Provide opportunities to solve the problem by suggesting possible solutions and allowing the teacher to create alternatives.
1. Identify the specific judgmental behavior that appears to be problematic.
2. Guide the teacher to see why it is critical to model a nonjudgmental attitude.
3. Collaborate with the teacher to define the attitude in specific terms and evaluate alternative strategies.
4. Provide encouragement to the teacher when you see evidence of successful strategy implementation.
5. Check back frequently on the progress and make adjustments as needed.

JUDGMENTAL

Structuring

Intervention Strategies

➢ **Ask Open-ended Questions**
Ask questions that provide for more than one simple answer, requiring the teacher to think more deeply about the behavior.
1. Ask questions such as "What happened? How did you react and what was the response of the other person? Why do you believe it was the other person's fault?" or "Was there any part of the situation that could have been your responsibility?"
2. Listen carefully and do not formulate the next question until you have paid attention to the answer for the first.
3. Encourage specific and relevant responses with appropriate follow-up questions such as "What could you have done differently?" and "How will you respond differently next time?"

➢ **Provide Alternatives**
Provide viable, appropriate options to the current inappropriate behaviors of the teacher.
1. Encourage the teacher to begin to recognize his or her judgmental attitude and ponder the use of more appropriate responses.
2. Collaboratively brainstorm realistic and specific alternative reactions to situations as they arise.
3. Help the teacher determine responses that might be perceived as less judgmental.
4. Have the teacher regularly touch base with you to discuss specific situations, how he or she reacted to them, and the results that followed.

JUDGMENTAL

Directing

Intervention Strategies

➢ **Ask "What" Questions"**
Ask "what" questions until the teacher acknowledges the action and volunteers a solution.
1. Begin by asking a "what" question such as "What evidence do you have that your point is correct?"
2. Continue asking "what" questions until the teacher stops making excuses and recognizes that the attitude is perceived as judgmental.
3. Follow up by asking "how" questions such as "How does making judgmental statements without all of the facts hinder communication?"
4. Ask another "what" question such as "What would a nonjudgmental response sound like?"
5. Establish a verbal agreement with the teacher to be cognizant of judgmental responses.
6. Monitor the teacher's responses to see if they improve, or if greater intervention is needed.

➢ **Provide Conflict Resolution**
Help the teacher resolve disputes through discussion and understanding and by jointly developing a resolution.
1. Identify the conflict caused by the teacher's perceived judgmental manner.
2. Describe the impact the judgmental attitude has on others.
3. Ask the teacher to describe his or her understanding of the issue.
4. Suggest ways the judgmental attitude can be diminished or eliminated.
5. Stay with the process until there has been acknowledgment of the judgmental attitude and the conflict diminishes.
6. Arrange to revisit the situation in a timely fashion to monitor progress.

LISTENING

Encouraging

Intervention Strategies

➤ **Check for Understanding**
To avoid the inappropriate behavior, have the teacher paraphrase the instructions ensuring understanding of your expectations.
1. In your discussions, ask questions frequently to discern the teacher's level of attentiveness to the conversation.
2. Have the teacher explain to you his or her understanding of what was discussed.
3. Encourage the teacher to listen intently reminding him or her how effective listening skills will improve performance and relationships.

➤ **Nonverbal Communication**
Use eye contact, body movement, or hand signals to gain the teacher's attention.
1. Physically acknowledge the inattention or lack of listening via raised eyebrows, a scowl, a shake of the head, or other appropriate body language.
2. Create a sense of community, respect, and care through nonverbal communication exhibiting your pleasure at seeing the teacher listen appropriately.
3. Physically acknowledge appropriate listening skills via a smile, a nod of approval, or a thumbs-up.

LISTENING

Coaching

Intervention Strategies

➤ **Brainstorm**
Assist the teacher in thinking through alternative approaches to improve the behavior.
1. Collaboratively brainstorm numerous alternatives to promote the teacher's improved listening skills.
2. Coach the teacher to identify two to three skills from the generated list that he or he believes could work.
3. Encourage the teacher to apply these skills and provide feedback of success.

➤ **Reflect Verbal Responses**
Verbally reflect the essence of a teacher's argument in order to clarify his or her true feelings regarding the situation.
1. In order to get the teacher to clarify underlying meanings, ask him or her, "If I hear you correctly, you are saying _____."
2. Listen carefully to the teacher's response and attempt to understand the underlying meaning.
3. Repeat the message back to the teacher and continue to seek clarity until he or she acknowledges his or her true feelings.
4. Ask the teacher what steps can be taken to ensure that his or her listening skills improve.

LISTENING

Structuring

Intervention Strategies

> **Ask Self-evaluative Questions**
> *Ask questions that cause the teacher to self-reflect on the behavior.*
> 1. At a regularly scheduled faculty meeting, distribute to everyone a self-assessment that includes questions directly dealing with the ability to listen to others.
> 2. When you see a teacher not listening to others, "befriend" him or her and model the type of listening skills that you would like to see displayed.
> 3. Look for opportunities to ask the teacher how he or she might feel if someone was not listening to his or her points.
> 4. Provide positive reinforcement when a positive response is elicited and gentle guidance of other alternatives if a negative response is received.

> **Provide Alternatives**
> *Provide viable, appropriate options to the current inappropriate behaviors of the teacher.*
> 1. Provide the teacher realistic and specific alternatives for improving listening skills.
> 2. Help the teacher determine which alternative might be more appropriate and in what circumstance.
> 3. Encourage the teacher to try some of the determined alternatives.
> 4. Have the teacher regularly touch base with you to discuss the successes and challenges he or she is having with the new listening strategies.

LISTENING

Directing

Intervention Strategies

> **Ask Convergent Questions**
> *Ask questions that allow for only very specific acceptable answers.*
> 1. Without allowing for excuses, ask for an explanation of why the teacher has difficulty listening.
> 2. Continue asking "why" questions until you arrive at what seems to be the root cause for the inattentiveness.
> 3. Ask the teacher to clearly identify steps he or she will take to increase attentiveness.
> 4. Monitor the implementation steps.

> **Redirect**
> *Stop the teacher's inappropriate behavior and refocus the attention to the task at hand.*
> 1. Call the teacher's attention to the lack of attention and how it is inappropriate.
> 2. Refocus the teacher's attention to appropriate listening skills that contribute to positive interpersonal relationships.
> 3. Clearly identify for the teacher what is expected.
> 4. Monitor the teacher and praise as needed, elaborating on the positive elements of the new behavior.

NEGATIVITY

Encouraging

Intervention Strategies

➤ **Affirmative Statements**
Verbally acknowledge and emphasize the teacher's strengths and achievements.
1. Highlight the positives in each situation.
2. Praise the teacher when he or she demonstrates a positive attitude.
3. Remind the teacher when he or she has previously demonstrated a positive attitude in a tough situation and encourage him or her to continue to do so.

➤ **Humor**
Use humor to lighten a stressful situation.
1. Use humor when a teacher is continually negative or overly serious.
2. Find ways to poke fun at yourself, allowing the teacher to understand you support him or her although you do not approve of the negative attitude.
3. Send a clear message that, although you are using humor to lighten the mood, you expect the teacher to demonstrate a positive attitude.

NEGATIVITY

Coaching

Intervention Strategies

➤ **Collaborate**
Have the teacher work together with others and self-assess how successful their solutions have been at solving the problem.
1. With the help of the teacher, clearly identify the perceived negativity.
2. Suggest that the teacher with the persistent negative attitude partner with a colleague within the building who has a much more positive nature.
3. Ask the teacher to tell you the specific differences between his or her attitude and that of the colleague.
4. Collaboratively determine what the teacher can and is willing to do to make appropriate changes.
5. Monitor progress and receive feedback regularly on the success of the solutions developed.

➤ **Guided Problem-Solving**
Provide opportunities to solve the problem by suggesting possible solutions and allowing the teacher to create alternatives.
1. Identify areas you have observed where the teacher demonstrates a positive attitude.
2. Discuss the concerns you have with the negativity.
3. Ask the teacher what he or she thinks is behind the seemingly poor attitude and what could be done to change it.
4. Relate the previously observed areas of strength to the issue of a lack of positive attitude highlighting the enthusiasm you have observed in other situations.
5. Work with the teacher to apply the skills he or she has demonstrated in other areas.
6. Provide encouragement to the teacher when you see evidence of more positive behavior.

NEGATIVITY

Structuring

Intervention Strategies

➢ **Persuade**

Use reasoning to help the teacher to understand the need for change.
1. Provide an environment that fosters a positive attitude.
2. Help the teacher believe what he or she does makes a difference.
3. State your specific concerns about the teacher's negativity.
4. Ensure the teacher understands the need to exhibit a more positive attitude.
5. Offer possible alternatives to the current behavior or attitude that would result in better relationships.
6. Follow up with the teacher to ensure the attitude is improving.

➢ **Provide Alternatives**

Provide viable, appropriate options to the current inappropriate behaviors of the teacher.
1. Provide clear expectations for a positive attitude and be sure they are understood by the teacher.
2. Facilitate goal setting for the teacher and provide periodic collaborative evaluations.
3. Schedule weekly classroom visits to look for improvement in attitude and to provide encouragement.

NEGATIVITY

Directing

Intervention Strategies

➢ **Ask "What" Questions**

Ask "what" until the teacher acknowledges the action and volunteers a solution.
1. Ask the teacher what affect he or she thinks his or her current attitude is having on them as well as others.
2. Give credibility to the teacher's feelings by affirming him or her even if you disagree.
3. Ask the teacher what ideas he or she may have of how to develop a more positive feeling about a person or situation.
4. Problem solve as necessary, affirming the teacher's feelings and efforts to find a resolution to the situation.

➢ **Directed Change**

Provide specific directives with the goal of changing the behavior and thus the results.
1. Identify the specific behavior that is negative.
2. Highlight how the teacher's attitude is causing concern.
3. Discuss with the teacher why a positive attitude is necessary.
4. Monitor and remind the teacher of the need for this change until he or she begins to develop a more positive attitude.

NONCOMPLIANCE

Encouraging

Intervention Strategies

> **Increase Physical Presence**
  Spend more time at the location where the problem behavior appears to occur most often.
  1. Arrange to be present in situations where the teacher's noncompliance typically arises.
  2. Position yourself near the locations at critical times where the teacher is assigned but may not be fulfilling duties.
  3. Frequently visit the classroom of the teacher who may not be following school and classroom policies and procedures.
  4. In the strategies above, verbal communication is usually not needed; your physical proximity and presence is often enough to change the behavior.

> **Nonverbal Communication**
  Use eye contact, body movement, or hand signals to gain the teacher's attention.
  1. Physically acknowledge noncompliant behavior via some type of nonverbal body language such as a raised eyebrow or a shake of the head.
  2. Create a sense of community, respect, and care through nonverbal communication exhibiting your pleasure at seeing the teacher comply with policies and procedures.
  3. Physically acknowledge compliant behavior via a smile, a nod of approval, or a thumbs-up.

NONCOMPLIANCE

Coaching

Intervention Strategies

> **Assisted Goal Setting**
  Help the teacher set achievable goals to improve behavior in a step-by-step manner.
  1. Reinforce the need to adhere to the policies and procedures and identify where the noticeable behavior falls short.
  2. Collaboratively brainstorm specific and realistic strategies in which the teacher can begin to comply with the policies and procedures.
  3. Establish a time frame in which these strategies and goals can be implemented.
  4. Providing feedback, periodically follow up with the teacher to ensure compliance and establish new goals if necessary.

> **Timely Identification of Inappropriate Behavior**
  Address the concerning behavior as soon as is reasonably possible in order to stop it from reoccurring.
  1. When you see the teacher display noncompliant behavior, privately bring it to his or her attention as soon as possible.
  2. Remind the teacher of more acceptable compliant behaviors that have been previously discussed.
  3. Be quick to acknowledge and affirm appropriate compliance.

NONCOMPLIANCE

Structuring

Intervention Strategies

➤ **Ask Self-evaluative Questions**
Ask questions that cause the teacher to self-reflect on the behavior.
1. At a regularly scheduled faculty meeting, distribute to everyone a self-assessment that includes questions directly dealing with noncompliance.
2. When you see a teacher not being compliant, "befriend" the teacher and model the attitude and/or behavior that you would like to see displayed.
3. Look for opportunities to ask the teacher how he or she might feel being on the receiving end of someone else's noncompliance.

➤ **Orchestrate Positive Peer Reinforcement**
Enlist fellow teachers to provide encouragement and affirmation for the teacher having difficulty.
1. Discuss with the teacher the issue of noncompliance and how it is affecting others.
2. Indicate that you'll be enlisting peers to encourage and affirm the teacher when he or she demonstrates compliant behavior.
3. Select peers to encourage and work with the teacher.
4. Follow up frequently with peers and the teacher to ensure more compliant behavior.

NONCOMPLIANCE

Directing

Intervention Strategies

➤ **Confront**
Directly address the inappropriate behavior being very specific about what is expected and what is not appropriate.
1. State specifically what the continuous noncompliant behavior is.
2. Review the steps needed to improve compliance.
3. Provide the teacher an opportunity to reply, but reiterate the problem and how it must be corrected immediately.
4. Closely monitor the teacher's progress toward the stated expectations and take alternative actions as necessary.

➤ **Redirect**
Stop the teacher's inappropriate behavior and refocus the attention to the task at hand.
1. Call the teacher's attention to the noncompliant behavior and why it is inappropriate.
2. Refocus the teacher's attention to positive behavior that contributes to appropriate compliance.
3. Clearly identify for the teacher what is expected.
4. Monitor the teacher and praise as needed, elaborating on the positive elements of the compliant behavior.

PARENT INTERACTION

Encouraging

Intervention Strategies

➤ **Check for Understanding**
To avoid the inappropriate behavior, have the teacher paraphrase the instructions ensuring understanding of your expectations.
  1. In your discussions regarding parent interactions, ask the teacher questions frequently to discern his or her level of knowledge regarding the issues that have come to light.
  2. In areas that seem unclear to the teacher, explain how to effectively use a variety of techniques for positively working and communicating with parents.
  3. Have the teacher explain to you his or her understanding of what was discussed.
  4. Ask the teacher to determine more positive ways to interact with parents.
  5. After the teacher has tried any new techniques for positively relating to parents, have him or her share with you what was learned from the experience and how it might be improved.

➤ **Encourage Confidence**
Provide positive statements about the teacher's ability to achieve success using examples from previous experiences.
  1. Identify areas where the teacher demonstrates confidence in his or her interaction with parents.
  2. Discuss the concerns you have and ask the teacher how he or she feels about those.
  3. Relate the previously observed areas of strength to the issue of poor interactions, pointing out the confidence you have observed in other situations.
  4. Work with the teacher to apply those skills to improve parent interaction.

PARENT INTERACTION

Coaching

Intervention Strategies

➤ **Reflect Verbal Responses**
Verbally reflect the essence of the teacher's argument in order to clarify his or her true feelings regarding the situation.
  1. Ask the teacher to tell you about specific parent interactions he or she had in the past that have been positive and those that have resulted in problems.
  2. Respond back to the teacher, restating the key issues you heard in the description.
  3. Ask the teacher if you have summarized correctly both the positives and the negatives.
  4. Provide the teacher with a list of potential alternatives for him or her to be more consistent in having positive parent interactions.
  5. Allow the teacher to choose from the list of alternatives and apply the most appropriate strategy.
  6. Have the teacher report back to you on the level of success of the new strategy and provide other alternatives as needed.

➤ **Timely Identification of Inappropriate Behavior**
Address the concerning behavior as soon as is reasonably possible in order to stop it from reoccurring.
  1. Discuss concerns that have come to your attention about negative parent interactions as soon as is reasonable.
  2. Provide opportunities for the teacher to make parent calls from your office so you can provide immediate guidance.
  3. Encourage teachers to keep a detailed log of parental contacts.
  4. Review the logs periodically and correct minor concerns when you see them during these reviews, maintaining a supportive approach.
  5. Acknowledge positive parent interactions with affirmative comments.

PARENT INTERACTION

Structuring

Intervention Strategies

➢ **Orchestrate Positive Peer Reinforcement**
Enlist fellow teachers to provide encouragement and affirmation for the teacher having difficulty.
1. Discuss with the teacher the issue of poor parent interactions and how they negatively affect students.
2. Indicate that you'll be enlisting peers to encourage and affirm the teacher when he or she demonstrates positive parent interaction.
3. Identify and assign exemplary teachers who exceed expectations in parental interactions to encourage and work with the teacher.
4. Meet with the pair to discuss experiences and highlight successes for both.
5. Follow up frequently with peers and the teacher to ensure that more positive interactions are occurring.

➢ **Provide Alternatives**
Provide viable, appropriate options to the current inappropriate behaviors of the teacher.
1. Collaboratively brainstorm realistic and specific alternative reactions to poor parent interactions as they arise.
2. Help the teacher determine which alternative reaction might be more appropriate when dealing with parents.
3. Encourage the teacher to begin accepting personal responsibility while pondering different alternative reactions.
4. Have the teacher regularly touch base with you to discuss specific parent interactions, how he or she reacted to them, and the results that followed.

PARENT INTERACTION

Directing

Intervention Strategies

➢ **Manage Anger**
Require the teacher to participate in anger management strategies.
1. Have the teacher identify what easily triggers his or her anger when dealing with parents.
2. Brainstorm alternative strategies to deal with anger when it arises.
3. Help the teacher to determine a safe place to "unload" away from parents when emotions intensify.
4. Follow up with encouragement, but if issues with managing anger continue, proceed to the next intervention strategy, "Outside Assistance."

➢ **Outside Assistance**
Coordinate help from an outside source with the specific skills needed to help address the issue.
1. Keep an accurate record of the specific problems you have observed related to poor parent interactions and identify outside resources to best assist the teacher.
2. Meet with the teacher to discuss your concerns and let him or her know of your intention to provide assistance.
3. Meet with the outside resource to discuss your concerns about poor parent interactions and your projected goals for the teacher and collectively determine the best strategy to approach the situation.
4. Permit the outside resource to work with the teacher.
5. Have the outside resource keep in touch with you to be sure that all are on the same page.
6. Follow up with the teacher to ensure that he or she is having more positive parent interactions and offer further assistance if necessary.

PLANNING SKILLS

Encouraging

Intervention Strategies

➤ **Affirmative Statements**
Verbally acknowledge and emphasize the teacher's strengths and achievements.
1. Praise the teacher when appropriate lesson plans are developed.
2. Find the positives, capitalizing on the strengths of the teacher and encouraging the use of those abilities.
3. Remind the teacher of when he or she has previously demonstrated appropriate planning and encourage him or her to continue to do so.

➤ **Modeling**
Demonstrate through example the behavior that is expected of the teacher.
1. Verbally acknowledge and praise good planning skills you have seen in others that the teacher should emulate.
2. Frequently praise exemplary planning skills in role models and monitor to see if this elicits similar behavior in the teacher.
3. Be quick to praise the teacher when he or she demonstrates appropriate planning skills.
4. Be consistent in your praise as the teacher begins to demonstrate appropriate planning skills.

PLANNING SKILLS

Coaching

Intervention Strategies

➤ **Assisted Goal Setting**
Help the teacher set achievable goals to improve behavior in a step-by-step manner.
1. Reinforce the need to develop good lesson plans to improve student learning.
2. Collaboratively identify specific and realistic planning goals the teacher can slowly begin to implement into his or her classes.
3. Establish benchmarks to monitor progress.
4. Provide feedback by periodically following up with the teacher to ensure proper lesson planning and establish new goals if necessary.

➤ **Timely Identification of Inappropriate Behavior**
Address the concerning behavior as soon as is reasonably possible in order to stop it from reoccurring.
1. Develop a paradigm of improvement rather than perfection.
2. Conduct 5–10 minute unannounced visits in the classroom and monitor the plans in an effort to provide improvement.
3. Have the teacher keep his or her lesson plans available when you come in, announced or not.
4. Maintain a supportive approach, correct minor concerns when you see them during these visits, but more importantly, be quick to acknowledge and affirm proper planning skills.

PLANNING SKILLS

Structuring

Intervention Strategies

➤ **Individual Accountability**
Identify the area of concern and allow the teacher to personally address it.
1. Speak to the teacher privately to avoid drawing undue attention to the lack of planning skills.
2. Ask the teacher what could be done differently in terms of lesson planning.
3. If necessary, provide possible suggestions for the teacher until an appropriate response is produced.
4. Praise the teacher's effort to plan appropriately and express your confidence when improvement is noted.

➤ **Provide a Timeline for Improvement**
Provide the teacher with a specific set of objectives for improvement that must be met along with clearly identified dates for attaining these objectives.
1. Identify specific and realistic objectives identifying how the teacher can improve planning skills.
2. Agree upon a time frame in which these objectives and goals can be implemented.
3. Provide feedback as each benchmark is addressed.

PLANNING SKILLS

Directing

Intervention Strategies

➤ **Confront**
Directly address the inappropriate behavior being very specific about what is expected and what is not appropriate.
1. State specifically what the continuous problem is.
2. Review the steps needed to improve lesson planning.
3. Provide the teacher an opportunity to reply, but reiterate the problem and how it must be corrected immediately.
4. Closely monitor the teacher's progress toward the stated expectations and take alternative actions as necessary.

➤ **Written Plan**
Develop a clear, concise plan for the teacher that contains specific goals and a timeline for achieving those goals.
1. Discuss with the teacher the most appropriate methods for planning.
2. Establish a systematic plan for improvement.
3. Sign a written agreement with the teacher that contains a specific timeline for implementation.
4. Monitor goal attainment, providing praise and revisions as appropriate.

RESENTFULNESS

Encouraging

Intervention Strategies

➤ **Humor**
   Use humor to lighten a stressful situation.
   1. Establish rapport and relationship with the teacher through appropriate humor, being careful to never be cutting or sarcastic.
   2. Find ways to poke fun at yourself to demonstrate similar times when you've been resentful in the past and how it was not productive.
   3. Send a clear message that, although you are using humor to lighten the mood, you are confident the teacher *can* demonstrate a nonresentful attitude.

➤ **Provide Feedback**
   Give a timely assessment regarding what the teacher is doing correctly and what needs to be improved.
   1. Speak to the teacher privately to avoid drawing undue attention to his or her resentful tendencies.
   2. Ask the teacher what could be done differently and provide appropriate suggestions where necessary.
   3. If needed, coach the teacher until an appropriate response is produced.
   4. Verbally acknowledge and praise positive responses.
   5. Be consistent in your praise until the teacher internalizes the desired qualities.
   6. Praise the teacher's effort to think through situations and express your confidence as improvement is noted.

RESENTFULNESS

Coaching

Intervention Strategies

➤ **Appeal to Values**
   Providing opportunity for self-reflection, discuss concerns and compare them to the positive values the teacher holds as demonstrated in the past.
   1. Gently remind the teacher of what he or she holds dear in terms of value.
   2. Inquire if the teacher thinks his or her resentfulness is appropriate.
   3. Have the teacher think about the attitude and identify a more appropriate response.
   4. Praise positive responses, and if there is a lapse in appropriate behavior, compare the reaction to his or her more typical positive behavior.

➤ **Timely Identification of Inappropriate Behavior**
   Address the concerning behavior as soon as is reasonably possible in order to stop it from reoccurring.
   1. When you see the teacher display resentful behavior, privately bring it to his or her attention as soon as possible.
   2. Remind the teacher of possible alternative behaviors that have been previously discussed.
   3. Be quick to acknowledge and affirm appropriate responses until resentfulness is significantly reduced.

RESENTFULNESS

Structuring

Intervention Strategies

➤ **Persuade**
Use reasoning to help the teacher understand the need for change.
1. Affirm your esteem for the teacher as part of the school and point out some positive contributions.
2. State your specific concerns about the teacher's resentfulness toward others.
3. Ensure the teacher understands the need to make changes.
4. Offer possible alternatives to the current behavior or attitude that would result in better relationships.
5. Continue the discussion until you have persuaded the teacher on at least one area where the attitude or behavior can improve.
6. Follow up with the teacher to ensure the attitude is improving.

➤ **Reflective Journaling**
Provide a journal for the teacher to reflect on the behavior and determine a more positive course of action in the future.
1. Discuss with the teacher the perceived resentfulness.
2. Ask the teacher to log his or her interactions with others and note where resentment might have surfaced.
3. In those incidents where the teacher believes the response may have been anything other than pleasant, have him or her reflect on ways the situation could have been handled better.
4. Have the teacher leave a margin on the right-hand side of the journal page for you to respond to the journal entry.
5. If the reflection is rather shallow, elicit additional thoughts and feelings in a nondirective manner until the desired level of understanding of the resentfulness is reached. This could be done in writing through the journal or in person.
6. Conclude interactions with encouragement and affirmation.

RESENTFULNESS

Directing

Intervention Strategies

➤ **Manage Anger**
Require the teacher to participate in anger management strategies.
1. Have the teacher identify if there is any underlying anger that triggers his or her resentfulness.
2. Brainstorm alternative strategies to deal with resentfulness when it arises.
3. Help the teacher determine a safe place to "unload" when emotions intensify.
4. Refer the teacher to outside assistance if the anger persists.

➤ **Provide Conflict Resolution**
Help the teacher resolve disputes through discussion and understanding and by jointly developing a resolution.
1. Identify the conflict caused by the teacher's perceived resentfulness.
2. Describe the impact the resentfulness has on others.
3. Ask the teacher to describe his or her understanding of the issue.
4. Suggest ways the resentful attitude can be diminished or eliminated.
5. Stay with the process until there has been acknowledgment of the resentfulness and the conflict diminishes.
6. Arrange to revisit the situation in a timely fashion to monitor progress.

SELF-CENTEREDNESS

Encouraging

Intervention Strategies

➤ **Affirmative Statements**
Verbally acknowledge and emphasize the teacher's strengths and achievements.
1. Praise the teacher when he or she demonstrates others-oriented behavior.
2. Emphasize the need to consider the needs of others.
3. Remind the teacher of when he or she has previously demonstrated others-oriented behavior and encourage him or her to continue to do so.

➤ **Assign a Mentor**
Assign the teacher a mentor who demonstrates the desired behavior.
1. Pair the teacher with a role model who is typically others oriented.
2. Have the teacher collaboratively work together on a project with the mentor modeling others-oriented behavior.
3. Check back frequently on the progress and make adjustments as needed.

SELF-CENTEREDNESS

Coaching

Intervention Strategies

➤ **Provide Leadership Opportunities**
Provide the teacher with opportunities to take on leadership roles related to the area of concern.
1. Assign the teacher to leadership positions on committees in areas of strength.
2. Coach the teacher on developing a leadership style that is particularly focused on the team.
3. Encourage the teacher to assume other leadership roles that will require him or her to listen and understand others' viewpoints.

➤ **Self-Disclosure**
Allow the teacher an opportunity to personally identify the issue and determine alternatives to resolve the problem.
1. Meet with the teacher to discuss what appears to be self-centered behavior in a particular instance.
2. Attempt to get the teacher to disclose the underlying reason why he or she may not be focusing on the needs of others.
3. Highlight the times when you have observed the teacher focused on the needs of others and the resultant positive outcomes.
4. Be quick to encourage and affirm others-oriented behavior.
5. Follow up by asking the teacher to reveal how he or she felt after demonstrating a more others-oriented behavior.

SELF-CENTEREDNESS

Structuring

Intervention Strategies

➤ **Ask Open-ended Questions**
Ask questions that provide for more than one simple answer, requiring the teacher to think more deeply about the behavior.
1. When trying to determine the reason for the self-centered behavior being demonstrated, ask questions such as "What are you doing now, that by doing it differently could better improve the situation?"
2. Follow up by asking "how" questions such as "How could you have focused more on others when you did _____?" or "How do you think you could do a better job at taking the needs of others into consideration?"
3. Ask another "what" question such as "What could you do differently in the future, and why?"
4. Establish a verbal agreement with the teacher of how he or she attends to be cognizant of others' needs in the future.
5. Monitor the teacher's attitude/behavior to determine if it improves, or if greater intervention is necessary.

➤ **Individual Accountability**
Identify the area of concern and allow the teacher to personally address it.
1. Speak to the teacher privately to avoid drawing undue attention to his or her lack of concern for the school and for others.
2. Ask the teacher to volunteer for school-sponsored projects or alternative activities that focus on the needs of others.
3. If necessary, coach the teacher until appropriate responses are produced.
4. Praise the teacher's effort for assuming individual responsibility and for being accountable in focusing on others.

SELF-CENTEREDNESS

Directing

Intervention Strategies

➤ **Confront**
Directly address the inappropriate behavior being very specific about what is expected and what is not appropriate.
1. State specifically the self-centered behavior that you have observed.
2. Provide the teacher an opportunity to reply, but reiterate the problem and how it must be corrected immediately.
3. Review steps needed to eliminate the self-centered focus of the teacher.
4. Closely monitor the teacher's progress toward the stated expectations and take alternative actions as necessary.

➤ **Redirect**
Stop the teacher's inappropriate behavior and refocus the attention to the task at hand.
1. Identify the self-centered behavior demonstrated by the teacher and explain why it is inappropriate.
2. Refocus the teacher's attention to positive behavior that contributes to the vision of the school and others.
3. Clearly identify for the teacher what is expected.
4. Monitor the teacher and praise as needed, elaborating on the positive elements when others-oriented behavior is demonstrated.

TECHNOLOGY

Encouraging

Intervention Strategies

> **Affirmative Statements**
  Verbally acknowledge and emphasize the teacher's strengths and achievements.
  1. Praise the teacher when he or she attempts to use new technology.
  2. Match the teacher with others who are willing to help and encourage him or her to most effectively integrate technology.
  3. Find the positives in the teacher's use of technology and encourage the continued use and expansion of those abilities.

> **Humor**
  Use humor to lighten a stressful situation.
  1. Establish rapport and relationship with the teacher through appropriate humor, being careful to never be cutting or sarcastic.
  2. Find ways to poke fun at yourself to demonstrate similar times when you've been technology shy in the past and how it was not productive.
  3. Send a clear message that, although you are using humor to lighten the mood, you are confident the teacher can successfully implement technology in the classroom.

TECHNOLOGY

Coaching

Intervention Strategies

> **Assisted Goal Setting**
  Help the teacher set achievable goals to improve behavior in a step-by-step manner.
  1. Reinforce the need to adhere to the technology policies and procedures and identify where the noticeable behavior falls short.
  2. Collaboratively brainstorm specific and realistic strategies in which the teacher can change his or her technology efforts.
  3. Establish a time frame in which these strategies and goals can be implemented.
  4. Provide feedback by periodically following up with the teacher to ensure the proper use of technology and establish new goals if necessary.

> **Collaborate**
  Have the teacher work together with others and self-assess how successful their solutions have been at solving the problem.
  1. With the help of the teacher, clearly identify the technology goal.
  2. Pair the teacher with others who have more experience in this area.
  3. Provide collaborative time in their schedules and a location for the pair to work.
  4. Monitor progress and receive feedback regularly on the success of any newly implemented technology initiative.

TECHNOLOGY

Structuring

Intervention Strategies

➢ **Provide Alternatives**
Provide viable, appropriate options to the current inappropriate behaviors of the teacher.
1. Collaboratively brainstorm realistic and specific situations when new technologies could be implemented to improve student learning.
2. Help the teacher determine which alternative might be more appropriate and when.
3. Encourage the teacher to try one new technology at a time in a subject area that he or she has the greatest experience teaching and is most comfortable with.
4. Have the teacher regularly touch base with you to discuss how the lessons turn out and the results that followed.

➢ **Provide a Timeline for Improvement**
Provide the teacher with a specific set of objectives for improvement that must be met along with clearly identified dates for attaining those objectives.
1. Identify specific areas in which the teacher can most effectively integrate the use of technology.
2. Together with the teacher, choose some appropriate ways to integrate technology and determine when and how they are to be used.
3. Agree upon a timeline for this technology integration and follow up on a scheduled basis to ensure implementation.

TECHNOLOGY

Directing

Intervention Strategies

➢ **Ask Closed Questions**
Ask questions that can normally be answered using a specific piece of information or a simple "yes" or "no."
1. Ask the teacher questions such as "Are you comfortable using the technology we have available?"
2. Ask the teacher if the lack of technology use in the classroom is in the best interest of the students.
3. Ask the teacher if he or she needs assistance to help become more familiar with when and how to do what is expected and provide assistance as needed.
4. Follow up to ensure the teacher is at least beginning to use technology in the classroom.

➢ **Outside Assistance**
Coordinate help from an outside source with the specific skills needed to address the issue.
1. Keep an accurate record of the specific technology issues you have observed and identify which outside resource would best assist the teacher.
2. Meet with the teacher to discuss your technology concerns and let him or her know of your intention to provide assistance.
3. Meet with the outside resource to discuss your technology concerns and projected goals for the teacher and collectively determine the best strategy to approach the situation.
4. Permit the outside resource to work with the teacher.
5. Have the outside resource keep in touch with you to be sure that all are on the same page.
6. Follow up with the teacher to ensure that he or she is appropriately integrating technology and offer further assistance if necessary.

TIME MANAGEMENT

Encouraging

Intervention Strategies

➢ **Affirmative Statements**
Verbally acknowledge and emphasize the teacher's strengths and achievements.
1. In faculty meetings and other faculty communications, let teachers know how much you value the efficiency that results from effective time management.
2. Praise the teacher when he or she efficiently manages time.
3. Remind the teacher of past accomplishments and successes that have stemmed from appropriate time management and encourage him or her to continue to implement those.

➢ **Nonverbal Communication**
Use eye contact, body movement, or hand signals to gain the teacher's attention.
1. Make eye contact with the teacher when you notice him or her not using the time in the classroom wisely.
2. Look up at the clock once they have seen you, as an indicator you have noticed the time.
3. Try to use twice as many positive nonverbal signals as negative ones. This tends to markedly increase appropriate responses. For instance, if the teacher begins to improve with time management, as you look at the clock, smile as well, or give a "thumbs-up."

TIME MANAGEMENT

Coaching

Intervention Strategies

➢ **Assisted Goal Setting**
Help the teacher set achievable goals to improve behavior in a step-by-step manner.
1. Reinforce the need for efficient and effective time management to improve student learning.
2. Collaboratively brainstorm specific and realistic goals in which the teacher can slowly begin to implement time management strategies into the day.
3. Establish benchmarks to monitor progress.
4. Provide feedback by periodically following up with the teacher to ensure more effective use of time and establish new goals if necessary.

➢ **Guided Problem-Solving**
Provide opportunities to solve the problem by suggesting possible solutions and allowing the teacher to create alternatives.
1. Work with the teacher to define the time management issue in specific terms (e.g., lessons continually running too long).
2. Focus on the specific problem so that the discussion doesn't get bogged down by other issues.
3. Guide the teacher to determine alternative techniques and strategies to more effectively use time in the classroom.
4. Help the teacher synthesize information and generate a plan for trying the new techniques.
5. Provide encouragement to the teacher when you see evidence of more efficient and effective use of time.

TIME MANAGEMENT

Structuring

Intervention Strategies

➤ **Individual Accountability**

Identify the area of concern and allow the teacher to personally address it.

1. Speak to the teacher privately to avoid drawing undue attention to his or her lack of time management.
2. Ask the teacher what can be done so he or she can more effectively manage time.
3. If necessary, coach the teacher until an appropriate response is produced.
4. Praise the teacher's effort to think through situations and express your confidence in him or her as improvement is noted.

➤ **Negotiate**

Work to reach a compromise with the teacher through open discussion.

1. Discuss with the teacher the need for improved time management.
2. Have the teacher explain clearly the issues he or she is having with time management.
3. Negotiate possible solutions to resolve the issue.
4. Follow up frequently to see if the negotiated agreement is being adhered to and determine if modifications are required.

TIME MANAGEMENT

Directing

Intervention Strategies

➤ **Ask Convergent Questions**

Ask questions that allow for only very specific acceptable answers.

1. Without allowing for excuses, ask the teacher to explain why time management is an issue.
2. Continue asking "why" questions until you arrive at what seems to be the root cause of the lack of time management.
3. Ask the teacher to clearly identify steps to more efficiently and effectively manage his or her time.
4. Monitor the implementation steps.

➤ **Written Plan**

Develop a clear, concise plan for the teacher that contains specific goals and a timeline for achieving those goals.

1. Discuss with the teacher the most appropriate strategies for improving time management.
2. Establish a systematic plan for improvement.
3. Sign a written agreement with the teacher that contains a specific timeline for implementation.
4. Monitor goal attainment, providing praise and revisions as appropriate.

WRITING SKILLS

Encouraging

Intervention Strategies

➤ **Assign a Mentor**
   Assign the teacher a mentor who demonstrates the desired behavior.
   1. Pair the teacher with a role model who excels in writing skills.
   2. Have the mentor and teacher collaboratively set goals for improving writing skills.
   3. Check back frequently to monitor progress and make adjustments as needed.

➤ **Modeling**
   Demonstrate through example the behavior that is expected of the teacher.
   1. Frequently acknowledge and praise good writing practices you have seen that teachers should emulate.
   2. Be quick to praise teachers when they demonstrate appropriate writing skills.
   3. Consider teaching a lesson for the teacher to demonstrate good writing strategies.
   4. Be consistent in your praise as the teacher internalizes the desired qualities.

WRITING SKILLS

Coaching

Intervention Strategies

➤ **Appeal to Values**
   Providing opportunity for self-reflection, discuss concerns and compare them to the positive values the teacher holds as demonstrated in the past.
   1. Provide opportunities for self-reflection related to the teacher's level of writing skill.
   2. Gently remind the teacher of what he or she holds dear in terms of value.
   3. Inquire if the teacher thinks his or her writing skills are at the level they need to be.
   4. Have the teacher think about how the lack of writing skills could be perceived in the community.
   5. Encourage the teacher to seek outside assistance to improve his or her writing.
   6. Follow up with praise when you notice an improvement in the writing.

➤ **Assisted Goal Setting**
   Help the teacher set achievable goals to improve behavior in a step-by-step manner.
   1. Reinforce the need to have good writing skills as a model for students to emulate.
   2. Collaboratively brainstorm specific and realistic goals to improve the teacher's writing.
   3. Establish benchmarks to monitor progress.
   4. Provide feedback by periodically following up with the teacher to ensure improvement and establish new goals as necessary.

WRITING SKILLS

Structuring

Intervention Strategies

➤ **Ask Self-evaluative Questions**
Ask questions that cause the teacher to self-reflect on the behavior.
1. When you see a teacher not meeting expected professional writing standards, inquire as to what is happening.
2. Ask the teacher what he or she would think if such writing appeared at their home.
3. Ask the teacher to self-evaluate and articulate the reasons why he or she is failing to meet expectations.
4. Compare the teacher's self-evaluation with your perceptions and together determine a plan for improvement.

➤ **Suggest Activities**
Provide a list of activities the teacher could use as an alternative in the future.
1. Suggest that the teacher partner with a colleague who displays exemplary writing skills.
2. Suggest a writing workshop for the teacher.
3. Have the teacher run every written communication either through a colleague you have selected who has exemplary writing skills or through you.

WRITING SKILLS

Directing

Intervention Strategies

➤ **Outside Assistance**
Coordinate help from an outside source with the specific skills needed to help address the issue.
1. Keep an accurate record of the specific problems you have observed related to writing concerns and identify which outside resource would best assist the teacher.
2. Meet with the teacher to discuss your writing concerns and let him or her know of your intention to provide assistance.
3. Bring in the outside assistance, discuss your concerns and projected goals, collectively determine the best strategy to approach the situation, and permit him or her to work with the teacher.
4. Have the outside resource keep in touch with you to ensure that all are on the same page.
5. Follow up with the teacher to ensure that he or she is working to improve his writing.

➤ **Written Plan**
Develop a clear, concise plan for the teacher that contains specific goals and a timeline for achieving those goals.
1. Discuss with the teacher the concerns related to his or her writing skills.
2. Establish a systematic plan for improving the teacher's writing to include outside assistance, workshops, or individual training as needed.
3. Sign a written agreement with the teacher that contains a specific timeline for implementation.
4. Monitor and revise the plan as necessary.

Chapter 10

Case Studies

This chapter provides two case studies for you to gain comfort in using the IISS before you actually implement it with your faculty.

CASE STUDY #1: BILL

Background

Bill is a ten-year veteran teacher and this year he has been transferred to Milk Lake Middle School. Bill has had a history of having difficultly relating to parents. He tends to be very frank and judgmental, and parents are put off by him. There have been several other principals with whom he has worked, and some have found ways to get him transferred out of their building.

This year Milk Lake Middle has a new principal, Ryan Parker. Mr. Parker has been a principal for five years and is known as a very compassionate leader who cares deeply about his staff. He treats everyone with a lot of sensitivity and the staff and parents have really responded well to him. Needless to say, Mr. Parker is a bit surprised by the way Bill interacts with parents, and even though it is early in the year, he has had several parent complaints regarding Bill. Mr. Parker knows that Bill has a history of being short and abrupt and seems to have no interest in getting along with the parents of his students.

The complaints to date have been generally that he has been rude on the phone and made it difficult to set up appointments to talk about student progress or to talk about ways to better help students. Mr. Parker knows that if he doesn't deal with Bill's interactions with parents, things will only get worse, so he decided that he should check out the IISS in the hope of finding a strategy that might be helpful.

Implementing the Individualized Intervention Strategy System

After completing the Stage of Motivation (Figure 10.1) and Behavior Style (Figure 10.2) checklists, Mr. Parker completed the Problem-Solving Worksheet (Figure 10.3)

153

and discovered that Bill had a Self-Assertive style and operated at the Self-Absorbed level, at least as far as parents were concerned. He then looked for the Problematic Issue of Parent Interaction on the Teacher Improvement Plan to determine at which level of intrusiveness to begin. To determine more specifically how to address Bill in a step-by-step manner, Mr. Parker then proceeded to review those listed under Directing from the Individualized Intervention Strategies to determine their appropriateness. Given that Bill had been transferred out of several schools because of poor parent interaction, Mr. Parker believed that probably the best way to deal with Bill would be to confront him using the Manage Anger (Directing) strategy.

Mr. Parker thought that rather than go to Bill's classroom to have the initial discussion, he would call Bill to his office, signaling that this wouldn't be a "getting to know you" meeting but instead something more formal. Once there, Mr. Parker asked Bill to sit down. Mr. Parker then began the conversation by saying that he had received several complaints from parents in the last several days. The complaints had occurred over a writing assignment on which many students had done poorly and Bill had written several disparaging remarks on the papers. Parents had reported that when they had tried to call Bill to schedule a meeting, he had been rude and made comments that essentially said their son or daughter knew what they did wrong and that he expected them to buckle down and to do better, and that, for now, there was no need for any type of parental meeting. In their offense, the parents had reported this to Mr. Parker.

Mr. Parker asked Bill if this was true, and Bill did not deny it, stating that the school had a lot of students who felt entitled and that he thought the best way to deal with them would be to lay it on the line and tell them he expected more from them. He said that as far as he was concerned, the parents who complained were "helicopter parents" and the sooner they quit hovering over their children, the better it would be for them.

Mr. Parker looked at Bill and took a deep breath. It was clear there was a difference in philosophy and Bill was very much adamant that his assumptions and actions were justified. Mr. Parker said, "Bill, I know you feel strongly about this and I am not going to try to change your mind, but you need to be aware that your response is not something I can endorse or overlook." He followed this with a question, "Bill, can you tell me what triggers your responses to parents when they call to inquire about the status of their child?" Bill rattled off things such as parents making excuses for their child and then accusing Bill of not doing his job well.

Mr. Parker then suggested they brainstorm alternatives to being rude or blowing parents off, recalling a strategy he learned for managing his own anger: self-talk. He said to Bill, "When you feel that you are about to get angry by something a parent said, what can you say to yourself that will cause you not to overreact?" Bill said, "Probably if I told myself that a blow out with the parent will not solve the problem and to stop and take a deep breath." Mr. Parker continued, "Okay, now if I am a parent like for example Mr. Jones who called you yesterday, what are some other ways you might respond to me when I ask about my son's status and progress." They talked for a few minutes and weighed several options that Bill could use. Mr. Parker was careful to say "you know there are some responses that I might feel comfortable with, but you won't. So, be up front with me and tell me the kinds of responses that make you uncomfortable and then tell me those you think you could learn to use." The meeting began to pick up positive speed, and between the two of them, they came up with some possible alternative strategies that Bill could use to satisfy the parents and to help the students, while helping Bill feel that he was setting the stage for the students to begin to do better.

Mr. Parker looked at Bill and said, "Okay fair enough, let's see if these new strategies will help begin to increase positive parent reactions, but if I see this problem continue and if I see you need some outside assistance, we'll get together again and talk things through. Fair enough?" Bill agreed and off he went.

Summary

Using the IISS, Mr. Parker had moved from the need for Bill to identify what triggered his anger to brainstorming possible alternative strategies to turn the situation around or to avoid them all together. Over the next several weeks, Bill made a concerted effort and things improved. Mr. Parker followed up and gave Bill a lot of encouragement when he got positive reports from parents. This seemed to be a turning point for Bill in terms of his teaching career. He may need other less intrusive approaches in the future, but the volatility of his behavior and the subsequent fallout definitely subsided.

Stage of Motivation Checklist

Teacher's Name: _____*Bill*_____   Date: _____

Stage 1 Self-Absorbed	Stage 2 Approval Oriented	Stage 3 Relationship Oriented	Stage 4 Others Oriented
✓ Usually wants his or her own way	___ Pursues certain subjects, activities, or hobbies in order to win approval	✓ Wants to be respected for his or her ideas	___ Seeks opportunities to help others
___ Has a very short attention span and changes activities often	___ Seeks attention	___ Loyal, standing up for family or friends	___ Often praises peers, even in their absence
___ Very possessive of his or her belongings	✓ Completes most tasks, but seeks verbal praise for his or her efforts	___ Even tempered and self-controlled	___ Self-motivated and enjoys feeling productive
___ Uses other people's belongings without asking permission	___ Seeks admiration for his or her achievements	___ Enjoys organized group activities	___ Volunteers for necessary tasks
✓ Becomes angry or resentful if opposed	___ Enjoys participating in competitive activities, but is upset if his or her efforts go unrecognized	___ Has a healthy appreciation of rules and group norms	___ Makes objective decisions
✓ Gets unusually upset when contradicted	✓ Judges others quickly, especially those whose achievements have been recently recognized	✓ Strives for competence	___ Converses with peers, administrators, parents, and students on their respective levels
___ Often must be told specifically what behavior is expected before he or she will comply	___ Behaves best when he or she is the center of attention	___ Enjoys being part of a particular group	___ Generally optimistic and resilient
✓ Has a low trust level, especially for those in authority	___ Loses interest in a task if not given constant attention and encouragement	___ Enjoys being associated with a group, organization, or team	✓ Stands up for his or her beliefs, even in the face of criticism
4 Total Checked	**2 Total Checked**	**2 Total Checked**	**1 Total Checked**

Figure 10.1

Behavior Style Checklist

Teacher's Name: _____*Bill*_____ Date: _____

Self-Assertive	Socially Interactive	Analytic	Accommodating
✓ Outspoken, opinionated, and assertive	___ Uses facial expressions and hand movements when talking	✓ Systematic and well-ordered, prefers to have a plan or method	___ Has an honest, low-key style
___ Active and resists staying in one place	✓ Expresses himself or herself well verbally	___ Seems very organized	___ Likes routine-is predictable and not quick to change
✓ Persistent-keeps pushing until goal is reached	___ Tends to be cheerful and sees the bright side of situations	___ Seems prepared for most events or activities	___ Seems mild tempered
✓ Decisive - makes decisions easily and sticks with them	✓ Persuasive - can present ideas convincingly	___ Tries hard to avoid unwanted surprises	___ Humble and modest about accomplishments
✓ Usually wins arguments or debates	___ Open-minded-open to others' ideas	✓ Seeks details	___ Compassionate-tends to be one of the first to help someone who is sick or hurting
✓ Tells people what he or she thinks	___ Friendly and outgoing	✓ Keeps records	___ Reserved around new people or in new situations
✓ Gets right to the point	___ Doesn't mind changing plans and is flexible	___ Restrained and usually very self-controlled, seldom loses temper	___ Takes time to think things through and get in touch with his or her feelings
___ Usually takes a leading role in a group	___ Enjoys being around people most of the time	___ Appears to be steady and calm	___ Tenderhearted-usually approaches people in a gentle, soft manner
___ Productive-works hard and gets a lot done	___ Likes change and diversity	___ Often critical of self	___ Empathetic-considers other people's thoughts and feelings
✓ Does not change mind easily once opinion has been formed	___ Highly verbal	✓ Prefers to thoroughly understand a new task or situation before trying it	✓ Prefers an organized environment with a minimum of unexpected change
✓ Likes to work independently and is able to do so effectively	___ Expresses affection and appreciation for others	✓ Approaches most problems in a logical fashion	___ Appears ready to defend and protect others, especially those in a weaker position
___ Competitive-strives to be first in most things	___ Is original-thinks of new and different ways to do things	___ Usually careful and tactful when communicating with others	___ Stable, acts sensibly and responsibly
___ Tends to be result oriented	___ Enjoys discussing goals and dreams	___ Thorough, often checking things multiple times	___ Usually calm, easygoing, and relaxed
8 Total Checked	**2** Total Checked	**5** Total Checked	**1** Total Checked

Figure 10.2

Problem-Solving Worksheet

Teacher's Name: _____*Bill*_____   Date: _____

<table>
<tr><th colspan="2"></th><th>Instructions</th></tr>
</table>

Instructions

Review the list of problematic issues and on the designated line below, enter the specific challenge for this teacher. Complete the Stage of Motivation and Behavior Style Checklists. Then in the table below, place a check mark at the intersection of this teacher's stage of motivation and behavior style. Simultaneously, go to the appropriate Teacher Improvement Plan that corresponds with the teacher's Behavior Style: Self-Assertive, Socially Interactive, Analytic, or Accommodating and on that table, find the problematic issue from the alphabetical list in the left hand column. Second, identify the teacher's stage of motivation (4, 3, 2, or 1). You will then go across the table where you will find four types of strategies based upon the needed level of intrusiveness: Encouraging (E), Coaching (C), Supporting (S), or Directing (D). Those at Stage 4 typically respond best from using the least intrusive or Encouraging strategies, while those at Stage 1 from the most intrusive or Directing. Once you have chosen the appropriate strategy type, go to the Individualized Intervention Strategies in chapter 9 where the problematic issues are listed alphabetically and are accompanied by two step-by-step strategies to assist you in changing the behavior.

Problematic Issue: _____*Poor Parent Interaction*_____

Stage of Motivation	Behavior Style			
	Self-Assertive	Socially Interactive	Analytic	Accommodating
Self-Absorbed	✓			
Approval Oriented				
Relationship Oriented				
Others Oriented				

Intervention Strategy: ____*Manage Anger*_____

Page Number:___139_____

Results: *Bill acknowledged what triggered his anger, collaboratively brainstormed possible alternative strategies to handling his emotions, and began to implement them. The parent complaints have subsided and Bill has made a decision to be more sensitive to parents and their inquiries. The test will come when Bill has to deal with a parent who is irate. Hopefully the new way of dealing with parents will be held together when dealing with a real angry parent.*

Figure 10.3

CASE STUDY #2: JULIE

Background

Julie has been at Williams Street Elementary School as a fourth grade teacher for three years and is seen by both parents and teachers as very effective and as one who brings a lot of joy and excitement to her classroom. She is a person who is easy to be around and she provides an exuberant atmosphere.

As much as the other teachers enjoy Julie, they prefer not to work with her on projects because she does not have a record of good follow-through, and when asked about why she hasn't completed a task, she will begin to shift blame to others. This results in hurt feelings and begins to tear at the cohesiveness of the staff. When Julie engages in this behavior, she will often begin to gather support for her lack of follow-through by complaining to others that she is not the one who dropped the ball. This has the effect of beginning to pit one teacher against another, which makes for a difficult working environment.

Sarah Ludvik, the principal for Williams Street Elementary, has just taken the helm this past year and was shocked when she began to notice the fallout from one of Julie's last projects. She saw the amount of hurt feelings that were generated by an episode of blame shifting that occurred the previous week and she knew this problem had the potential to continue to get worse and to further eat away at the unity of the school staff if intervention was not provided. The problem was how to deal with the issue.

Implementing the Individualized Intervention Strategy System

After completing the checklists for the Stage of Motivation (Figure 10.4) and Behavior Style (Figure 10.5), Ms. Ludvik completed the Problem-Solving Worksheet (Figure 10.6) on Julie in order to identify what could be done. She believed that Julie was Socially Interactive and the checklists confirmed that. As she looked at the Stages of Motivation checklist, Ms. Ludvik realized that Julie generally operated on Stage 3 or 4, but when faced with any hint of criticism or if she felt pressured, her level could easily drop to Stage 2 or even Stage 1. This presented Ms. Ludvik with a problem: how do you deal with someone who operates on a high level most of the time but when confronted or pressured will sink to very low levels and then become defensive and possibly even vindictive? Looking at Blame Shifting on the Socially Interactive Teacher Improvement Plan, Ms. Ludvik determined she had multiple strategies from which to choose, several of which looked promising: checking for understanding, asking open-ended questions, asking "what" questions, and possibly even providing conflict resolution if she thought this was necessary.

Given the tension that existed within the staff, Ms. Ludvik didn't think conflict resolution would work because Julie would probably consider it an attack on herself, at least at this time. It was Ms. Ludvik's thought that maybe using several strategies together might be the best way to deal with Julie.

Ms. Ludvik determined that Julie would probably operate at stage two, the approval level, while interacting with her, because she had not been a participant in the project in which the behavior occurred. Based on that assumption, Ms. Ludvik determined that she would start out by using the open-ended questions approach (Structuring) to begin the conversation with Julie and then move to the "what" questions (Directing) if Julie began to provide excuses. She thought if Julie got to the point where she was assuming some responsibility for her actions, maybe helping her to reframe (Coaching) her responses might be useful.

Ms. Ludvik found a time at the end of the day when all of the students were gone and the school was pretty quiet. She went down to Julie's classroom and poked her head in and asked, "How are things going, Julie?" Julie responded with a tentative "Fine," which gave Ms. Ludvik a clue that Julie was expecting some kind of confrontation. Ms. Ludvik asked if they could sit down and talk and Julie said "Sure" and cleared a spot for Ms. Ludvik at one of the reading tables. Ms. Ludvik said that she had become aware that there had been some conflict among several of the teachers regarding the project they were working on and she asked, "Could you tell me what happened?"

Julie proceeded to give Ms. Ludvik her version of the incident and clearly protected herself by shifting blame to Mary, one of the other fourth grade teachers. Ms. Ludvik followed up by saying, "Why do you think that this was Mary's fault?"

Julie launched into an elaborate reason for blaming Mary, and Ms. Ludvik listened carefully and then switched over to the "what" questions phase by saying, "Let me understand this a little better. What were your responsibilities in this project?" After getting more info from Julie, including hearing that Mary didn't tell Julie when her part was due, Ms. Ludvik said, "What were Mary's responsibilities? What did you do when you realized that you hadn't been told of your due date?" Julie responded by saying, "Well, I just figured that they either didn't need my part or they would tell me when it was time for me to begin."

Ms. Ludvik said, "What has been the result of the conflict?" Julie told her that it had caused bad feelings and that she had been unfairly blamed.

Ms. Ludvik then said, "In retrospect, what could you have done differently to have avoided this confrontation?" Julie replied, "Well, I could have actively tried to find out when my part was due." Ms. Ludvik agreed and then moved to reframing by saying, "I understand how you might feel you were unfairly blamed but when you use the initial response of blaming others, what do you think that does?" Obviously Julie knew that she shouldn't have blamed others for the problem but she said, "Well, they were making me feel it was all my fault." Ms. Ludvik asked, "How might you have gotten your message across without blaming them for the mess up, because I really don't believe that was your intention, was it?"

Julie responded by saying, "No, I just don't like to be blamed for something I didn't do on purpose."

Ms. Ludvik said, "Okay, how do you think you could have handled this differently?" Together, they agreed that she should have clarified when her due date was. Secondly, they talked about how blaming others doesn't really solve the issue but instead creates a toxic work environment. Then they discussed how she might have reframed some of her responses to the others in a manner that wouldn't worsen the situation. Finally, they talked about what she might do to lessen the tension with the others.

Julie took the meeting to heart and went to the others to apologize for her behavior, acknowledging how she overacted and basically said she valued their relationship too much to let it go up in smoke over something that occurred because she hadn't taken the initiative in finding out her due date. Since that time, Julie has been less defensive and has on occasion gone to Ms. Ludvik and asked her how to handle other sensitive issues.

Summary

Using the IISS, Ms. Ludvik continued to periodically touch base with Julie in a nonthreatening way, gently probing to ensure that things were moving in the right direction. Julie's behavior had moved from shifting blame to others for her lack of follow-through to not only accepting responsibility for the tasks required of her but also completing them in a timely fashion. This greatly improved Julie's relationships with her colleagues, greatly diminishing the conflict that had previously ensued making for a much more collegial environment within the grade level.

Stage of Motivation Checklist

Teacher's Name: _____ *Julie* _____ Date: _____

Stage 1 Self-Absorbed	Stage 2 Approval Oriented	Stage 3 Relationship Oriented	Stage 4 Others Oriented
___ Usually wants his or her own way ✓ Has a very short attention span and changes activities often ___ Very possessive of his or her belongings ___ Uses other people's belongings without asking permission ✓ Becomes angry or resentful if opposed ___ Gets unusually upset when contradicted ___ Often must be told specifically what behavior is expected before he or she will comply ___ Has a low trust level, especially for those in authority	___ Pursues certain subjects, activities, or hobbies in order to win approval ✓ Seeks attention ___ Completes most tasks, but seeks verbal praise for his or her efforts ✓ Seeks admiration for his or her achievements ✓ Enjoys participating in competitive activities, but is upset if his or her efforts go unrecognized ✓ Judges others quickly, especially those whose achievements have been recently recognized ✓ Behaves best when he or she is the center of attention ___ Loses interest in a task if not given constant attention and encouragement	✓ Wants to be respected for his or her ideas ___ Loyal, standing up for family or friends ___ Even tempered and self-controlled ___ Enjoys organized group activities ___ Has a healthy appreciation of rules and group norms ___ Strives for competence ✓ Enjoys being part of a particular group ✓ Enjoys being associated with a group, organization, or team	___ Seeks opportunities to help others ___ Often praises peers, even in their absence ___ Self-motivated and enjoys feeling productive ✓ Volunteers for necessary tasks ___ Makes objective decisions ___ Converses with peers, administrators, parents, and students on their respective levels ✓ Generally optimistic and resilient ___ Stands up for his or her beliefs, even in the face of criticism
__2__ Total Checked	__5__ Total Checked	__3__ Total Checked	__2__ Total Checked

Figure 10.4

Behavior Style Checklist

Teacher's Name: _____ *Julie* _____ Date: _____

Self-Assertive	Socially Interactive	Analytic	Accommodating
___ Outspoken, opinionated, and assertive	✓ Uses facial expressions and hand movements when talking	___ Systematic and well-ordered, prefers to have a plan or method	___ Has an honest, low-key style
___ Active and resists staying in one place	✓ Expresses himself or herself well verbally	___ Seems very organized	___ Likes routine-is predictable and not quick to change
___ Persistent-keeps pushing until goal is reached	___ Tends to be cheerful and sees the bright side of situations	___ Seems prepared for most events or activities	___ Seems mild tempered
✓ Decisive - makes decisions easily and sticks with them	✓ Persuasive - can present ideas convincingly	___ Tries hard to avoid unwanted surprises	___ Humble and modest about accomplishments
___ Usually wins arguments or debates	___ Open-minded-open to others' ideas	___ Seeks details	___ Compassionate-tends to be one of the first to help someone who is sick or hurting
___ Tells people what he or she thinks	✓ Friendly and outgoing	___ Keeps records	___ Reserved around new people or in new situations
___ Gets right to the point	___ Doesn't mind changing plans and is flexible	___ Restrained and usually very self- controlled, seldom loses temper	___ Takes time to think things through and get in touch with his or her feelings
___ Usually takes a leading role in a group	✓ Enjoys being around people most of the time	___ Appears to be steady and calm	✓ Tenderhearted-usually approaches people in a gentle, soft manner
___ Productive-works hard and gets a lot done	___ Likes change and diversity	___ Often critical of self	✓ Empathetic-considers other people's thoughts and feelings
___ Does not change mind easily once opinion has been formed	✓ Highly verbal	___ Prefers to thoroughly understand a new task or situation before trying it	___ Prefers an organized environment with a minimum of unexpected change
___ Likes to work independently and is able to do so effectively	___ Expresses affection and appreciation for others	___ Approaches most problems in a logical fashion	___ Appears ready to defend and protect others, especially those in a weaker position
✓ Competitive-strives to be first in most things	___ Is original-thinks of new and different ways to do things	✓ Usually careful and tactful when communicating with others	___ Stable, acts sensibly and responsibly
___ Tends to be result oriented	✓ Enjoys discussing goals and dreams	___ Thorough, often checking things multiple times	✓ Usually calm, easygoing, and relaxed
2 Total Checked	**7** Total Checked	**1** Total Checked	**3** Total Checked

Figure 10.5

Problem-Solving Worksheet

Teacher's Name: _____*Julie*_____ Date: _____

Instructions

Review the list of problematic issues and on the designated line below, enter the specific challenge for this teacher. Complete the Stage of Motivation and Behavior Style Checklists. Then in the table below, place a check mark at the intersection of this teacher's stage of motivation and behavior style. Simultaneously, go to the appropriate Teacher Improvement Plan that corresponds with the teacher's Behavior Style: Self-Assertive, Socially Interactive, Analytic, or Accommodating and on that table, find the problematic issue from the alphabetical list in the left hand column. Second, identify the teacher's stage of motivation (4, 3, 2, or 1). You will then go across the table where you will find four types of strategies based upon the needed level of intrusiveness: Encouraging (E), Coaching (C), Supporting (S), or Directing (D). Those at Stage 4 typically respond best from using the least intrusive or Encouraging strategies, while those at Stage 1 from the most intrusive or Directing. Once you have chosen the appropriate strategy type, go to the Individualized Intervention Strategies in chapter 9 where the problematic issues are listed alphabetically and are accompanied by two step-by-step strategies to assist you in changing the behavior.

Problematic Issue: _____*Blame Shifting*_____

Stage of Motivation	Behavior Style			
	Self-Assertive	Socially Interactive	Analytic	Accommodating
Self-Absorbed				
Approval Oriented		✓		
Relationship Oriented				
Others Oriented				

Intervention Strategy: _____*Ask Open-Ended Questions*_____

Page Number:____85_____

Results: *Julie began to take responsibility for her actions and became aware of how she was coming across. She apologized to fellow faculty members and since has become less defensive and has assumed responsibility for her actions.*

Figure 10.6

References

Calfee, R. (2006). Educational psychology in the 21st century. In P. Alexander & P. Winnie (Eds.). *Handbook of Educational Psychology* (2nd ed.). New York, NY: Routledge.

Collet, V. S. (2012). The gradual increase of responsibility model: Coaching for teacher change. *Literacy Research and Instruction, 51,*27-47.

Collins, J. (2001). *Good to great: Why some companies make the leap...and others don't. New York, NY: Harper Business.*

Cooper, J. M. (Ed.). (2003). *Classroom teaching skills* (7th ed.). Boston: Houghton Mifflin.

Glickman, C. D., Gordon, S. P., & Ross-Gordon, J. M. (2012). *The basic guide to supervision and instructional leadership* (3rd ed.). Boston: Pearson.

Gregorc, A. (1979). Learning and teaching styles: Potent forces behind them. *Educational Leadership, 36,* 234-236.

Harris, A. (2009). *Distributed leadership: Different perspectives.* London, England: Springer.

Hersey, P. & Blanchard, K. (1982). *Management of organizational behavior: Utilizing human resources* (4th ed.) Englewood Cliffs, NJ: Prentice-Hall.

Levine, A. (2005). Educating school leaders. *The Education Schools Project.* Retrieved from http://www.edschools.org/pdf/Final313.pdf

Marston, W. M. (1979). *Emotions of normal people.* Minneapolis, MN: Persona Press.

McEwan, E. K. (2005). *How to deal with teachers who are angry, troubled, exhausted, or just plain confused.* Thousand Oaks, CA: Sage.

Ribas, W. B. (2005). *Teacher evaluation that works.* Westwood, MA: Ribas Publications.

Schon, D. A. (1996). *Educating the reflective practitioner: Toward a new design for teaching and learning in the professions.* San Francisco: Jossey-Bass.

Selig, G., & Arroyo, A. (1989). *Loving our differences: Building successful family relationships.* Virginia Beach, VA: CBN Publishing.

Selig, W. G., & Arroyo, A. A. (1996). *Handbook of individualized strategies for classroom discipline.* Los Angeles: Western Psychological Services.

Selig, W. G., Arroyo, A. A., Lloyd-Zannini, L. P., & Jordan, H. (2006). *Handbook of individualized strategies for building resiliency in at-risk students.* Los Angeles: Western Psychological Services.

Selig, W. G., Arroyo, A. A., & Tonkin, S. E. (2009). *Handbook of individualized strategies for building character.* Los Angeles: Western Psychological Services.

Sullivan, S. & Glance, J. (2005). *Supervision that improves teaching.* Thousand Oaks, CA: Corwin Press.

Index

About the Authors

Dr. George Selig has served at Regent University since 1980 in various leadership roles: professor of special education, dean of the College of Education and Human Services (later renamed the School of Education), provost, and, for the last decade, as professor and Distinguished Chair of Educational Leadership in the School of Education. Prior to his arrival at Regent, he was a teacher, coach, and acting principal both in Alaska and in Massachusetts as well as director of Special Education and director of Pupil Services in Northampton and Longmeadow, MA. Simultaneously, he taught part-time at Smith College in Northampton. During that time, he provided valuable leadership in developing the Massachusetts law protecting the rights of the handicapped. As a result, he was awarded a Washington Fellowship to develop policy papers to be used in implementing the Federal Law for the Handicapped (P.L. 94-142). Dr. Selig is the author of *Training For Triumph* (1984), a book on child-rearing and lead coauthor of multiple books over the last twenty-five years: *Loving Our Differences* (1989), a family development and communication manual; *Handbook of Individualized Strategies for Classroom Discipline* (1995); *Handbook for Building Resiliency in At-Risk Students* (2005); *Handbook of Individualized Strategies for Building Character* (2009); *Loving Our Differences for Teachers* (2010), and *The Secret Kingdom for Educators* (2011). George and his wife, Judy, reside in Virginia Beach, VA. They have two daughters, four grandchildren, and two great grandchildren.

Dr. Linda Grooms currently serves as professor and chair of the post-master's programs in the School of Education at Regent University. Prior to her arrival at Regent, she was a high school band director in SC and an elementary guidance counselor and K–6 building administrator in Virginia Beach City Public Schools. With almost three decades of leadership experience and degrees in both educational and organizational leadership, she has a passion for nation-building through the transformation of educational systems and the leaders who serve them. In addition to her university teaching, she conducts leadership training both nationally and internationally, while continuing her longitudinal research of the ontology, epistemology, and axiology of leaders and their consequent development of those they serve. Linda resides in Chesapeake, VA.

Dr. Alan Arroyo served in several roles at Regent University from 1986 to 2015: professor, director of Academic Services, and dean of the School of Education. In addition, he codirected several projects to train educators on how to teach character in public schools funded by the United States Department of Education, the Virginia Department of Education, and several foundations. Before coming to Regent University, he was a teacher and administrator in Illinois public school systems specializing in Special and Alternative Education. Currently he is the director of the School of Education at Clarion University of Pennsylvania. Dr. Arroyo has made over 100 professional presentations and coauthored over 15 books, some of which are *Loving Our Differences* (1989), *Handbook of Individualized Strategies for Classroom Discipline* (1995); *Handbook for Building Resiliency in At-Risk Students (2005); Handbook of Individualized Strategies for Building Character (2009); Loving Our Differences for Teachers* (2010), and *The Secret Kingdom for Educators* (2011). With his wife, Susan, Alan calls Virginia Beach, VA home. They have four children and 10 grandchildren.

Dr. Michael Kelly is a clinical associate professor at Virginia Tech, where he teaches in the educational leadership program. Prior to his tenure as an associate professor, Mike was a principal and teacher in the Virginia Beach City Public School System, where his school was identified as a "School to Watch" by the National Middle School Association. Mike resides in Virginia Beach, VA, with his wife. Amy, and their two daughters, Maddie and Gail.

Dr. Glenn Koonce is currently an associate professor at Regent University and chair of the Educational Leadership programs in its School of Education. Prior to his arrival in the field of education, he was a highly trained and highly decorated combat squad and platoon leader with the First Air Cavalry Division in Vietnam during 1970–71. Dr. Koonce has been a teacher, coach, principal, and central office administrator in the public schools as well as a visiting scholar at Virginia Tech University and the George Washington University. In addition, he has served as an adjunct professor at the George Washington University and Old Dominion University, where he directed the Tidewater Principal's Center. Among his many achievements and awards are "Principal of the Year" for the Commonwealth of Virginia, President of the Virginia Association of Secondary School Principals (VASSP), "Boss of the Year" several times in Chesapeake Public Schools, and "Professor of the Year" for the School of Education at Regent University. Dr. Koonce has been the president of the Virginia Education Research Association (VERA), chairman of the Virginia Education Coalition (VEC), and president of the Virginia Professors of Educational Leadership (VPEL). Dr. Koonce is a Board Certified Auditor for the Virginia Department of Education (VDOE) and Lead Auditor for the Council of Accreditation for Educator Preparation (CAEP). He also serves on the Board of Editors for the National Council of Professors of Educational Administration (NCPEA) and reviewer for the Center for Scholastic Inquiry (CSI). Glenn resides in Chesapeake, VA, with his wife, Suzanne.

The most challenging and rewarding achievements of **Dr. Herman Clark** career took place when he was principal of Bowling Park Elementary School. There, the students and parents were cooperative, supportive, and committed to education. The old African American proverb was deeply rooted in the community of Bowling Park School: "It takes a village to raise a child." The church, scouts, recreational leaders, businesses, etc., were active participants in teaching these students. When Bowling Park scored in the top five on the state achievement test, it proved what can happen when the school and community work together. Under Dr. Clark's leadership, parents were totally involved in the school voicing their opinions, speaking at local, state and national PTA conferences, and seeing to it that they reinforced those concepts and skills the teachers were trying to cultivate in the classroom. The students were excited about learning and were always eager to "show off" their intellectual ability. The entire staff served as MOMS and DADS to all students. In 1997, Dr. Clark was promoted to assistant superintendent of Norfolk Public Schools and continued working with schools and community in improving student achievement until his retirement in March 2004, when he joined Regent University as an assistant professor. Herman is married to Dr. Reuthenia Clark, principal of Azalea Middle School in Norfolk, VA, and Founder of the Ministry School of Music, Inc. They have two children, Johanna Joy, a surgical assistant in Atlanta, GA, and Dr. Victor Pierre, internal medicine physician at Sentara General Hospital in Norfolk, VA.